— THE —
CREATIVE TOOLKIT
FOR WORKING WITH
GRIEF AND
BEREAVEMENT

A Practitioner's Guide
with Activities and Worksheets

Claudia Coenen

Jessica Kingsley Publishers
London and Philadelphia

The epigraph on page 9 is reproduced from *It's OK that You're NOT OK* © 2017
Megan Devine used with permission of publisher, Sounds True Inc.

The bullet list on page 45 is reproduced from Wolfelt (2003) *Understanding
Your Grief: Ten Essential Touchstones for Finding Hope and Healing Your
Heart* in line with the Companion Press permissions policy.

The epigraph on page 49 is reproduced with kind permission from Moke Mokotoff.

The epigraph on page 57 is reproduced from *It's OK that You're NOT OK* © 2017
Megan Devine used with permission of publisher, Sounds True Inc.

The epigraph on page 58 is reproduced with kind permission
from Victoria Zaitz—www.victoriazaitz.com.

The epigraph on page 59 is reproduced with kind permission from Eben Coenen.

The epigraph on page 67 is reproduced from *Glad No Matter What* ©2010 SARK. Reprinted
with permission by New World Library, Novato, CA—www.newworldlibrary.com.

First published in 2020
by Jessica Kingsley Publishers
73 Collier Street
London N1 9BE, UK
and
400 Market Street, Suite 400
Philadelphia, PA 19106, USA

www.jkp.com

Copyright © Claudia Coenen 2020
Illustrations pp.95–103 by Masha Pimas

Library of Congress Cataloging in Publication Data
A CIP catalog record for this book is available from the Library of Congress

British Library Cataloguing in Publication Data
A CIP catalogue record for this book is available from the British Library

ISBN 978 1 78775 146 0
eISBN 978 1 78775 147 7

Printed and bound in the United States

The Creative Toolkit for Working with Grief and Bereavement

Contents

INTRODUCTION

When I was 15, I wrote in my journal that I wanted to live my life as creatively as possible. I had already been performing folk music with my family since I was nine, and we were about to record our second album. I had been studying dance for 12 years and was presenting my own choreography in concerts at my school. An avid reader, I enjoyed the journey to other worlds through books, poetry, and plays, especially Shakespeare, whose works I read aloud with Opa, my German grandfather. Opa took me to the opera, to plays, and musicals. He seemed to be a walking dictionary who would include the derivation and root language of any word I asked him the meaning of. We rode the subway to museums where Opa explained paintings and sculptures along with a history lesson about the artist.

My parents participated in community theater and had many friends who were actors, musicians, and dancers. Our travels as a folk singing band connected me with other performers, many of whom were activists as well. My best friend Deborah came from a creative family as well. Her mother was an opera singer and her father was a prolific artist. Creativity was an integral part of my life, and artistic expression enhanced and informed it.

That aspiration in my journal was a statement of how I wanted to live. I wanted to be able to respond to events, emotions, and the people I engaged with in a creative manner. It meant that I would make music and dance, that I would continue my habit of processing my internal world in a series of journals. And since our music had a socially responsible component, I believed that by living creatively, by connecting with different people around the world, by continuing to read and learn, I would become a better person, and when I had children, I would be able to guide them intelligently and creatively on their own life journeys.

I met my future husband, Albert George Coenen, Jr, or Alby, as we affectionately called him, by answering a newspaper ad seeking roommates. Once I moved to New York City to pursue my dance career, we began to date and eventually married. He is the father of our three children, my partner, my companion, and my counterpart. At least he was. He died of a sudden heart attack in May 2005, four days after his 50th birthday.

Alby's death sent me into a tailspin. It seemed as if my life shattered into pieces around me. Reaching for a new journal, I scribbled my shock, pain, anger, and sense of abandonment on every page. I filled 12 books in the first year. I also used embroidery, music, collage, crayons, and paint to release my sorrow, and even danced out my grief. My creativity offered me a framework in which to process my grief, to mourn his death, and to slowly figure out how to live again.

I returned to school for a degree in Transpersonal Psychology which aligned with a quest for wholeness after the shattering of death. My training as a counselor and thanatologist has broadened my ability to respond to clients from different demographics, and my life experience enables me to respond with kindness to my clients. But it was Alby's life that generated a yearning to help others.

This book offers information on grief and how to help grieving clients. The activity sheets in Part Two are useful tools that can help the bereaved explore their loss in creative ways, which might activate more emotion but ultimately provide an invitation to go deeper into their experience. Creativity can carry you through to another level of understanding, one that is expressed in color, shape, and imagery. I invite you and your clients to explore creative possibilities for healing.

All pages marked with ✖ can be photocopied and downloaded from https://library.jkp.com/ redeem using the voucher code GYOTEKE

PART ONE

We have to start telling the truth about this kind of pain. About grief, about love, about loss.

Because the truth is, in one way or another, loving each other means losing each other. Being alive in such a fleeting, tenuous world is hard. Our hearts get broken in ways that can't be fixed. There is pain that becomes an immovable part of our lives. We need to know how to endure that, how to care for ourselves inside that, how to care for one another. We need to know how to live here, where life as we know it can change, forever, at any time.

We need to start talking about that reality of life, which is also the reality of love.

Megan Devine

Chapter 1

WHAT IS THANATOLOGY?

Thanatology is the study of death, dying, and bereavement, named after the god, Thanatos, who is often depicted as the Angel of Death. Thanatos assisted his brother Hypnos, the god of sleep, in assuring a peaceful death, guiding a soul to the afterlife gently. Thanatos is such a minor god in ancient mythology that I cannot find him in my *Bulfinch's Mythology* (Bulfinch 1963), another book my grandfather gave me when I was interested in gods and goddesses as a young person. Thanatos is also depicted as the Grim Reaper, who appears when it is someone's "time" to die. This image expresses the fear of death that has permeated human thought and been a focus of religious explanations for generations. How do we understand death? How, if we do not understand it, can we help those who suffer after the death of someone close?

The field of thanatology addresses this inquiry—how we die and how we grieve. Thanatology also includes care for the dying and help for the bereaved, and encompasses research into the psychology of loss. Grief counselors strive to provide sensitive, culturally attuned assistance to their bereaved clients. Hospice professionals and End of Life Doulas assist dying people, helping them to make decisions about the circumstances surrounding their death, and also helping family members with important conversations. Just as a Birth Doula assists a pregnant woman in developing a birth plan and provides guidance during the birth, an End of Life Doula helps a terminally ill patient plan their death, and might even enable them to create legacy projects or write letters to their family members to be read after their death. Doctors, nurses, and palliative care and hospice workers may not call themselves thanatologists, but they are often skilled, compassionate practitioners who know how to keep a dying person comfortable and also to simply be present at the time of death. They are able to witness the pain of the people who are close to these patients, providing emotional as well as physical comfort. They do not try to heroically prevent death; instead, end of life professionals facilitate as much peace as they can for the patient and for family members.

Thanatology is the science of the relationship between the living and the dead, and how life is impacted by death. Everything that lives will die and we all will experience loss multiple times during the course of our lives. As practitioners, the more we know about how loss affects people, the more information we will be able to draw from in order to help our clients. From Sigmund Freud's old observation (1953) that we can simply replace one object of affection with another, through an understanding of how different attachment styles affect degrees of reaction to loss, thanatological research continues to study and report nuances that enhance our understanding of grief. We have come a long way from the thought that we merely need to "get on with life" or move through a certain number of "stages" to finish up with grief and get back to normal. Now we recognize that this is neither a realistic nor even a healthy approach. We cannot return to life as it was before any more than we can return to childhood whenever we wish to. We are forever changed by loss, and while this may feel daunting and painful, there are elements within loss that can stimulate us to move forward through our lives and to continue to live well.

A bereaved person does not forget about the one who has died, and nor is there any set way to grieve. There is no definite amount of time in which grief is completed, and it is not necessary to pretend to feel fine, and nor is it essential to forget, to put the past behind as if it has no impact on the present or the future. We now recognize that loss affects human beings on all levels. While emotional reactions are most obvious, there are also cognitive, social, physical, and spiritual responses.

I am a thanatologist and grief is my specialty. People come to my office grieving the death of someone significant, sometimes years after the loss. Since there is often grief in other situations, I also see clients who are affected by a divorce or break-up, or who may have received a diagnosis or are coping with terminal illness themselves. I help people who are experiencing grief symptoms in anticipation because someone close to them is ill and may die. My understanding of grief in its myriad manifestations enables me to assist these clients. I continue to learn and apply new models developed through research in bereavement, a field that has interested psychologists, physicians, philosophers, and thanatologists for more than a century, perhaps even since humans have lived, died, and been mourned.

ABOUT THIS BOOK

If you are a therapist or counselor, or someone who works with people experiencing trouble in their lives, chances are that these clients will bring grief along with their stories. Whether you work with couples dealing with relationship issues or your practice is trauma informed, whether you are an addiction counselor or a nurse on a maternity ward, it is likely that you will encounter grief. New parents, holding their tiny bundle, hours old, might tear up because of the death of a parent recently or even years ago, suddenly realizing how much they miss this person who will never get to hold this baby. Trauma and addiction have deep roots in grief as these issues often relate to abuse, neglect, and other adverse childhood experiences. There is grief when things do not go as planned; there is grief when people divorce. There can be grief at transitional times in life such as enrolling in a new school, moving to a new locale, or changing careers. Not everyone will have a strong, emotional grief response to these transitions, but many do. People who seek psychological help for these issues often have a history of small and large events in their past, many of which could fall under the umbrella of grief.

Having an understanding of loss, how it affects living, and how to help clients who are coping with it is important. Yet grief is largely ignored in psychological or medical training. Just as people are now realizing that it is important to talk about death and mortality, it is equally important that practitioners have more than a 50-year-old, often misunderstood, "model" to offer clients.

This book presents several current models of bereavement in use today. This is by no means an exhaustive list, but these are the models I am most familiar with, and the ones that I find most effective with my own clients. This book also contains ideas that you can use with your own clients. The models and activities provide a springboard to deepen the conversation in our counseling offices and to allow the bereaved to discover insights, consider memories, and express their pain. In addition, given the inevitable tension between feeling and doing, these activities give clients something to do, which in turn gives them hope that they will be able to clarify their feelings and apply their discoveries to their own healing. Having a question to contemplate can lead them to journal their thoughts, which in turn gets those spinning thoughts out of their heads and on to a page. Encouraging clients to tell their story in different ways helps them stimulate shifts and even transform their stories and how they feel about what has happened.

Please visit the Resources section at the end of the book to learn more about thanatology and the creative process from practitioners who work with grieving clients, conduct research, write books and offer trainings, lectures, and workshops.

WHAT NOT TO DO

No guide to helping grieving clients would be complete without a caution. Before I offer my own warnings, I want to address a central question that almost all grievers ask—how long will grief take?

There is no real answer to this question, although there are a lot of opinions on this subject. Adages such as "time heals all wounds" may be helpful to some but make no sense to others. And how much time are we talking about anyway? Psychological standards such as the DSM (*Diagnostic and Statistical Manual of Mental Disorders*) have tried to clarify this question for diagnostic purposes, which unfortunately brings normal grieving into a pathological realm. Is grief "resolvable" in six months? A year? Three years? When do outsiders, including doctors, therapists, friends, or co-workers, lose patience with the person in grief who is struggling, not only with the emotional, cognitive, and even financial changes in their lives, but also with changes in their status and identity?

Rose Kennedy, a woman who experienced much grief in her life, commented, "It is said 'time heals all wounds.' I do not agree. The wounds remain. In time, the mind, protecting its sanity, covers them with scar tissue and the pain lessens. But it is never gone" (Rose F. Kennedy 1974).

Others say that grief cannot be put aside, but we can learn to carry it. Art therapist Sharon Strouse, grieving the death of her 17-year-old daughter, says:

> In the early days, right after Kristin's suicide, I was told by survivors, "In time, there will be healing." I was not reassured by that thought. I couldn't imagine myself or my future in the face of her violent death. Ten years later I had a different perspective. There *was* healing, a healing shaped by the choices I made. Each day was up to me. My rational mind directed me at first. Eventually my heart opened to a journey that made healing possible. (quoted in Strouse 2013, p.201; original emphasis)

Note that Sharon speaks about healing that has taken a decade to sink in. She is not talking about being "healed;" rather, she finds herself on the long road to seeing it as a possibility. This is a reminder for all of us that each person's grief takes as long as it takes. I have worked with widows who are devastated by the death of their spouse for four or five years. People who have lost a child may find their intense grief lasts much longer. Conversely, I recently met with a woman whose husband died shortly before his 100th birthday. She acknowledged that she missed him, but she also wondered if there was something wrong with her because she had not cried or grieved too much. She said she felt that his life had been a complete one and that made her happy when she thought about him.

It is imperative that we allow our clients to grieve at their own pace. This may be frustrating at times as we witness what looks like "improvement" only to see them slip backwards into longing and sorrow over and over. This is how grief sometimes flows, up and down, back and forth. Witness it. Support it. Let it be.

Here are few things that practitioners should avoid:

- Make sure that you do not have an agenda with a timetable for your client's grief process. Grief takes its own time, which is probably longer than you or the client thinks.

- Try to avoid giving advice or attempting to "fix" their grief. Death cannot be fixed. The emotions, ranting, longing, and wishing for their lives to settle down or get back to "normal" need validation, not dismissal. Once they have explored their reaction to these issues, you can help them process their feelings and gradually guide them towards reinvesting in life. Do not suggest that they just keep busy or put it behind them. Do not tell them how to feel or what to do.

- Self-disclosure of your own losses can help sometimes, but this is a bit tricky. If you have experienced a similar loss or you understand grief from the inside, sharing some of how you coped might help a client see that they, too, can get through this. A griever may actually relax and open up if they know that you, too, have experienced loss. But if you share too much, the session will become more about you and less about them, so please be careful.

- Please do not offer clichés or platitudes that you think would be soothing. Other people, less sensitive than you, are already doing that. Take my word for it, bromides do not help.

- Allow for crying, venting, and even some panic attacks. Empathize and support, even if your clients' emotional distress is uncomfortable for you. See the somatic activities in Part Two for ideas on how to help clients soothe after they are finished crying.

- Don't suggest that there is a right way to grieve; there is not. What works for one person may not work for another, and what worked last session for this client may not be the right approach in this session. The process of grieving is very unruly and changeable. Be prepared for your client's reactions to change as they move backwards and forwards, up and down on the emotional roller coaster.

WHAT YOU CAN DO

- Compassionate presence, active listening, and reflection are the best tools you have when a client exhibits acute grief. Support, validation, and sympathy go a long way in soothing emotional expression, which needs to take place before any strategies can be offered or skills enhanced. Listen. Observe. Facilitate. Allow time for insight to bubble up amidst the tears. Open your own heart and create a safe space for your clients to experience all aspects of their grieving.

- Take care of yourself. Notice if grief from your own life is being triggered. Be aware of personal agendas, impatience, and judgment, and try to set these aside until the session is over. If you are activated personally, journal for yourself. Talk with a colleague or a therapist of your own so that you can approach each client with clarity and warmth.

Chapter 2

EARLY ROOTS

Sigmund Freud identified the difference between grieving and depression in his 1917 paper, "Mourning and Melancholia," which is what depression was referred to in Freud's time.[1] In his view, a person develops a close relationship with another that becomes a bond, or a "cathexis." When this relationship ends due to death, the person experiences many emotions such as sadness, longing, lack of interest in the world, and inability to see the future. The difference is that in melancholia, the patient also exhibits extreme lack of self-regard, and there does not seem to be an obvious event that caused the melancholia. With mourning, the loss of the love interest causes the emotions that appear similar to melancholia. Freud believed that mourning, over time, would resolve itself.

> Mourning is regularly the reaction to the loss of a loved person, or to the loss of some abstraction which has taken the place of one, such as one's country, liberty, an ideal, and so on. In some people the same influences produce melancholia instead of mourning and we consequently suspect them of a pathological disposition. It is also well worth notice that, although mourning involves grave departures from the normal attitude to life, it never occurs to us to regard it as a pathological condition and to refer it to medical treatment. We rely on its being overcome after a certain lapse of time, and we look upon any interference with it as useless or even harmful. (Freud 1953, p.243)

Freud observed that mourning took place in the conscious mind because the person knew that a loss had taken place. In his view, once the person had experienced all the emotional aspects of mourning, they would be able to set aside the love object and "decathect" from the dead person. This would then allow them to continue to live and to perhaps find a different "object" to love.

While this view seems simplistic now, it is important to recognize that Freud was the first person to write about the distinction between what looks like similar emotional reactions. While we now know that it is often not possible to just stop thinking about someone who has been important and influential in our life, and nor is it required,

---

1   See www.freud.org.uk/2017/11/11/mourning-melancholia-life-face-loss

Freud was not incorrect in his view that many grievers will be able to resolve their feelings about loss over time by engaging in grief work.

Following up on Freud's work, early psychologists not only differentiated between depression and the emotions of grief; they also began to study the psychological implications of a person's mental well-being when confronted with loss and tragedy. World War I left multitudes of injured, traumatized people in its wake, including women who had been brought up to get married only to find the marriageable prospects either dead or maimed. In Britain alone, there were two million "surplus women" after the war, many of whom had lost fiancés, husbands, or potential partners. The grief of entire populations was discounted, pushed aside with an attitude of "getting on with life" and not giving in to the "weakness" of sorrow.

Also during World War I, medical professionals began to understand that blast brain injuries were real and not tantamount to a lack of "moral fiber" when thousands of soldiers returned from the trenches, not only physically devastated, but also mentally incapacitated. This syndrome was originally called shell shock, and is now referred to as post-traumatic stress disorder (PTSD). Research and study in thanatology looked deeper into why some people react to grief differently than others, and psychologists began to apply attachment theory to how human beings cope with loss and with disasters, both man-made and natural.

Practitioners now have a large compendium of science, psychological research, and information to draw upon in order to help people who are grieving. Since most normal grief situations will indeed resolve over time, grief counseling is often a short-term intervention in which the counselor supports the emotional expression and helps the bereaved recognize connection, resilience, strengths, and skills so that they can figure out how to live fully again after loss. Sometimes this includes working with some historical losses and understanding the family values, dynamics, and cultural ways of coping with loss. Sometimes grief work simply helps the client move through, rather than get stuck in, their loss. Each person is unique. It is our job as practitioners to be open to our clients' needs, to help them discover their own path on their personal grief journey.

THE FIRST BIG GRIEF STUDY

In 1942, in the city of Boston in the USA, fire broke out late at night at the Cocoanut Grove nightclub. The Grove, as the nightclub was referred to, was packed with double its normal capacity, with over 1000 people inside, since this was a big sports weekend and people were celebrating. Local men and women, college students, and Navy personnel were among the partiers. As the fire began to spread, there were not enough exits available for the people inside. Patrons rushed for the doors and many were trampled in the melee, overcome by smoke or burned in the firestorm.

Firefighters responded quickly but did not have enough resources to deal with the blaze. The club was in the Boston Navy Yard and many inside the club were sailors. The

Navy, the Coast Guard and the Boston Police all joined the firefighters to help with the inferno. Harvard Medical School provided doctors, nurses, medical students, hospital orderlies—basically, anyone who was able to assist. They clawed through the wreckage to remove wounded people, carry out the dead, and begin the daunting task of identification. Many of the women in the nightclub had been separated from their handbags and it was very difficult to identify them. Police and college personnel pored through housing lists at Harvard and at Radcliffe College to try to discover who was missing.

The entire city of Boston was in shock. The Cocoanut Grove fire took the lives of 492 people, the largest death toll of one event in the continental US until 9/11. A total of 114 burn victims were rushed to Massachusetts General Hospital, where psychiatrist Erich Lindemann was the chief of psychiatric outpatients. In order to treat the burns, doctors began to come up with innovative techniques but were puzzled by their patients' reactions to their attempts to help them. Some patients were angry, belligerent, and uncooperative. The doctors thought that something else besides their burns was affecting their patients, and they called on Dr Lindemann to evaluate what it was.

In talking with the angry and highly distressed patients, Lindemann discovered that all of them had lost someone in the fire. They were, in fact, suffering from acute grief. Lindemann worked with these survivors for a long time, developing ways to help them, and observing their reactions to their losses. Having previously worked with patients who had lost an organ or a limb, Lindemann likened bereavement to losing a body part, and made the connection between the distress over this kind of radical change and the distress over losing a person who is important to your life. He documented physical symptoms such as throat tightness and sighing and cognitive symptoms such as ruminations and flashback, auditory hallucinations where the bereaved person would hear their loved one calling out to them. Some seemed to embody the personalities of their loved ones and others experienced survivor's guilt. Lindemann believed that his work could help the survivors work through their acute distress, adjust to life without them, and slowly learn how to re-engage in their own lives.

Lindemann's paper on his observations, "Symptomology and Management of Acute Grief" (1944), provides a basis for work in crisis management and trauma. His was the first longitudinal study of grief, and his work cracked open a door to recognizing that the emotional and psychological distress of acute grief can be treated (Rosenfeld 2018).

GRIEF TODAY

What do you know about grieving? Do you think there is a certain time in which one should be finished with it? Have you grieved in your own life? How have you personally processed loss? What is an "acceptable" way to grieve? Are you uncomfortable with the idea of death, yet find that sometimes a grieving client might seek your help? What skills will you draw upon to provide this assistance? What have you learned about death, dying, and bereavement?

The problem is, the research into how we grieve and how we heal is not included in training programs for psychologists, doctors, nurses, mental health counselors, or other types of therapists. If there is any discussion of grief, typically the only model mentioned is Elisabeth Kübler-Ross's five stages of grief (see the Resources section at the end of the book). This theory has taken hold in popular culture—it pops up in television shows, in books, and in newspaper articles on grief. The five stages have wormed their way into everyday conversations and are put forth as if they are a codified method to get through the pain of losing someone. It's as if society is saying that if you start at the first stage and go through all of them to the fifth stage, you have done your grief work—fix your grief in five easy steps and boom, move on. Applause, applause, you are finished. Now you can forget and get on with your life.

Listen carefully.

There are no stages of grief. You may have heard of them and think they represent *the way to grieve.* Kübler-Ross wrote her first book 50 years ago and it was a snapshot of 200 dying patients, not about grief at all! If you needed surgery, would you be comfortable with a doctor who only practiced techniques that were 50 years old?

There are no stages, there is no one way to get through. Each person is unique, each relationship is distinct, and each person's grief is also just that, uniquely their own. As practitioners who will undoubtedly encounter grieving clients, we need to know about current research in the field of bereavement. We need to have a metaphorical box of useful models and a variety of approaches so that we can offer a flexible response to our different clients.

The overview of research contained in this book is offered to stimulate you to learn more about grief and the field of thanatology. Please visit the Resources section at the end of the book for a list of books you can read to learn more.

Part Two of this book is a section of creative activities that you can use with your clients. These are flexible and can be used to address cognitive, emotional, and physical aspects of grief. I offer them so that you can have an assortment of tools to help your clients with their different responses to loss. I also invite you to bring your own wisdom and your own unique way of working with your clients to help them navigate their loss and to figure out how to live fully again, as best they can.

WHAT ABOUT YOUR OWN GRIEF?

We practitioners are human beings and have our own personal histories of relationships, ways of thinking, and our own traumas and losses. Many therapists and counselors are drawn to the field precisely because they themselves have suffered in some way. I wouldn't be a grief counselor if it were not for my own widowhood.

While our own lives can inform how we counsel others, it is also important to take our own reactions to another person's story out of the picture. This is not always a simple directive, for our experiences give us the ability to sympathize and understand something of what our client is going through, and it is often from this place of shared connection that a therapeutic alliance arises. Yet our clients come in to our offices in order to figure out how to live with what life has thrown at them. The counselor's job is not to be a fixer or even (in most cases) an advisor. This is an edge we must carefully navigate when a person comes in with a story that touches something similar to our own. It is imperative that we remain sympathetic but not judgmental, open to another's possibly quite different reaction to a similar event.

Being aware of our own inner responses and reactions is very important here. As we listen, watching for cues from the client, we must also be aware of what is happening within us. Are we tensing up? Are we closing off in some way? Are we leaning back and crossing our arms, or are we sitting in an open way, receptive to the expressions of our client? Are we breathing calmly as we talk with them? And what is coming up for us, knocking, as it were, on the inner door of our own awareness?

It would be a good idea to take a look at your own loss history so that you understand what might be triggered. Working with the grief of others invariably touches on our own and we need to be prepared. There are many ways you can do this, but I have created a simple timeline that can be used for this purpose—see Part Two for the "Loss History" activity.

By observing your own relationship with death, you might notice how different losses have affected you in different ways depending on how old you were and who it was. You might notice what you learned from those people in your life who died, and if you have incorporated or rejected some of those influences. Don't judge; just notice. Be informed by your own losses so that you can be open to those of a bereaved client who comes to you for help. If you have suffered a recent loss, use this timeline to prepare yourself and how you might react if your own grief arises during a session with a client.

Chapter 3

CREATIVITY

Throughout my life, I have engaged in debates about whether or not creativity is inherent in humans. Certainly some people seem to be born with talent or even prodigious abilities. Others don't exhibit what we normally think of as creative aptitude; some even claim that they "don't have a creative bone" in their body. While genius is rare and most people who express themselves creatively are not Picasso, Ai Weiwei, or Martha Graham, or have the ability to become a famous artist, I actually believe that all human beings are creative. If we stop thinking about a painting that is worthy of exhibition in a museum or being able to perform well in front of hundreds of people, we can look at creativity in a smaller yet more natural way. That flash of insight that comes from seeing a situation in a new way is creative thought in action. Communicating a story to someone in a way that makes it come alive for your listeners is a creative act. Singing a lullaby while snuggling a baby opens the baby both to love and to the feeling music evokes, even if you forget the words and are not completely tuneful. Preparing a pleasant meal, serving it nicely, and enjoying it with others is also an expression of creativity, whether you followed a recipe to the letter or invented something new. Arranging your furniture in a new way that is pleasing to you is also an act of creativity. Planting a garden, writing a nicely worded condolence or congratulatory note—these also require some creativity.

Merriam Webster defines "creativity" simply as "the ability to create." The *Oxford English Dictionary* defines it as "the use of the imagination or original ideas to create something: inventiveness." So, when we use our imagination, we are being creative even if there is no product to show for it. When creativity is used to manage difficult life events, the experience is often richer and deeper.

The concept of using creative process for healing is an ancient one. In ancient Greece, people went to dream temples to work through difficulties in their lives, using their imagination and dreams to heal themselves with the guidance of the temple attendants. Shamans in primitive cultures used sound, masks, dance, and other creative techniques to rid the body and mind of disease. Modern-day art therapists are skilled in allowing their clients to use multiple artistic media to develop personal insight or to express deeper truths and awareness. Expressive writing has been proven to help work through and release held emotions and can even alleviate traumatic reactions. My own instinctive way of helping myself through the trauma of loss has an actual basis in therapeutic practice.

In his book, *Trust the Process: An Artist's Guide to Letting Go*, Shaun McNiff writes about creative process. He says:

> The discipline of creation is a mix of surrender and initiative. We let go of inhibitions, which breed rigidity, and we cultivate responsiveness to what is taking shape in the immediate situation. The creative person, like the energy of creation, is always moving. There is an understanding that the process must keep changing. (McNiff 1998, p.2)

These ideas of a mixture of surrender and initiative offer a creative way of looking at grief. The bereaved person surrenders to the emotionality of loss and also discovers what to do with their grief and how to cope with it. Exploring grief through creative process enables the griever to tap into their imagination, where one might find "an ongoing interplay between many different and often contradictory elements" (McNiff 1998, p.2). Grief is like that; one minute you are feeling calm and relatively normal and the next, you are doubled over in sorrow and anguish. The use of color, imagery, sound, movement, and word helps to broaden the experience, allowing the griever to integrate those contradictory elements. McNiff suggests that we trust this creative impulse without trying to produce a work of art or to direct what arises too much. He says that there is an intelligence and an energy to creativity:

> The notion of "process" suggests a multiplicity of components with independent ways. But the word also carries within itself a sense of unity, a faith that all of our experiences gather together in a creative process that ultimately knows where it needs to go. (McNiff 1998, p.4)

While McNiff is not talking about grief, he is talking about the benefits of using creative process. And working through a grief experience is indeed a process. I believe that when we apply creative thought, creative activity, and expression to pain, distress, and even tragedy, we have a broader opportunity to engage with the process, move through it, and ultimately find ways to heal.

CREATIVE PROCESS

Kenneth A. Doka is a psychologist, thanatologist, and professor who teaches about dying and bereavement. His work has influenced how we think about grief as he has evaluated cultural influences and losses that are often not acknowledged. He coined the term "disenfranchised grief" which covers those losses that are harder to see, such as miscarriage, infant loss, and stigmatized relationships. His ideas on styles of grieving are discussed along with the dual process model in Chapter 4. In his book, *Grief Is a Journey* (2016), Doka explains why using creative expression can help the bereaved:

Expressive approaches work because they are natural. You are using a common activity to express what you are experiencing. These approaches are reflective—allowing you to explore fully your reactions. These approaches are cathartic—releasing pent-up energy as you engage in the activity. They draw from your inner self—connecting you to your culture, background and beliefs. Finally, they work... (Doka 2016, p.100)

Creative techniques, accessible to everyone
JOURNALING

Writing is an excellent way to process life experiences, especially difficult ones. Expressing yourself through writing can be done on a pad of paper, loose leaf, on index cards, or in a bound book. Writing in a journal does not have to be approached as a daily log of activities, as in "Dear Diary, today I had oatmeal for breakfast." No matter what medium is used, a private journal is a container for thoughts, feelings, dreams, lists, quotes from poetry, or lyrics. The journal can contain musings as well as doodles or drawings. Photographs or other mementos can be pasted in.

Expressing your inner world through writing is a proven way to work through issues. In the 1980s, James Pennebaker conducted studies of college students to see how expressive writing affected their ability to succeed in school. He instructed them to write for a set period of time, every day, for four days. Some students were asked to write about random daily events and others were asked to write about an incident in their lives that was emotionally activating. The students who wrote about difficult events had a marked increase in grades after the experiment. Pennebaker and his researchers observed a reduction in stress levels, an increase in function, and many other benefits in this experiment. The studies looked at physiological changes as well as reported reactions to the writing experiments (Pennebaker 1997).

Behavior can be affected by expressive writing. By venting and processing traumatic events in writing, students in Pennebaker's study exhibited the ability to think more clearly:

Expressive writing is a self-reflective tool with tremendous power. By exploring emotional upheavals in our lives, we are forced to look inward and examine who we are. (Pennebaker and Evans 2014, p.21)

Pennebaker observed that people seemed to become healthier in general when they engaged in expressive writing. Writing about emotional events in their life improved the overall health of subjects, no matter their age. Expressive writing was shown to reduce adverse emotional states such as anxiety and depression. It is in this way that journaling through grief can help the writer express how they feel and to work through some of the emotions they are experiencing.

Similar studies have been conducted in research labs since Pennebaker, who continued to conduct experiments, lecture, and write about his findings. His work is referred to as the "Pennebaker Paradigm" in subsequent writing experiments.

Journaling can also include letters written to the deceased. This is a useful way for the griever to cope with things they wish they had said. They can tell their loved one about their lives in their journal and use the book as a way to express thoughts and feelings they wish to convey, even though the recipient is no longer present. If they wish, they can read their letter at the graveside, if that is meaningful to them. Another technique is for the griever to write back to themselves in the voice of the deceased. Alexandra Kennedy's book, *The Infinite Thread*, contains many exercises for dialoguing with the deceased through writing and imagination (see the Resources section at the end of the book).

The journal can also be a repository for inspiration. Lyrics of a meaningful song can be placed in the journal or photographs can be pasted in. Poetry or inspirational quotes can find a place in a journal and can provide comfort and encouragement.

The metaphor of the journal as a container is a beneficial one. People in grief can spend a lot of time ruminating, which interferes with daily life and often causes sleep problems. By spilling their spinning thoughts out onto the pages of a journal, the writer can then close the book and place it on a shelf, metaphorically setting those thoughts aside for a while.

COLLAGE

"Why don't you make a collage?"

The bits of paper I endlessly touched allowed me to come to terms with the past, the present, and the future. I discovered myself in the process. I glued myself down and did not blow away. There was forgiveness. I collaged and wrote my way through it all. I breathed my way through and got very, very still. I listened. I learned to live in the moment. Living in the present allowed me to surrender my future; it will be what it is. I have embraced life and found purpose. I found meaning. It was an artful grief. (Strouse 2013, p.258)

In my office, I keep folders containing clippings pulled from a variety of magazines such as travel, fashion, gardening, art catalogs, sports, and psychology. I have colored tissue paper and origami paper with various designs. I keep a separate folder with words and phrases in it. In advance of a collage activity, a client might be invited to bring in some pictures that are important to them to use in their collage.

Collage can be done on a piece of paper or on a sturdier surface such as cardboard. I purchase rounds that are meant to serve as cake bases, which come in many different sizes. These are also useful for tracing shapes on paper for clients to use. Once I have presented the materials, I invite clients to look through the clippings and to choose images that seem to pop out. Some therapists keep stacks of magazines for this purpose—clients flip through a few magazines and cut out the pictures they want to use. Clients may find a page where one part of the image speaks to them and then they can use scissors to cut out the part they want. Another approach is to rip the picture out. Torn edges can become a metaphor for loss as clients piece together the chosen images to create a new picture, a whole view of how they are feeling in the moment.

Collage can also be done on a box. Cigar boxes or empty shoe boxes are useful for this, and craft stores often sell plain boxes that can be painted or collaged on. This can become a memory box that can hold special items from the deceased. This activity is a good one to use with bereaved children, but it is also effective for adults. Making memory boxes after a person has died can also be a family activity.

DRAWING

Creative process is not about making a piece of art, suitable for display. Sometimes it is hard for a client to get beyond thinking about the end result of what they are creating. I often see bereaved people who actually are artists in real life, and it is particularly challenging for them to let go of the concept of the outcome or a finished work. Encourage clients to let go of what it looks like and to settle into the process. They might close their eyes or use a non-dominant hand to break free of the "goal" and drop into the exploration.

Using artistic modalities allows the client to engage with color, form, and shape, and these inform the senses, opening up a realm of feeling rather than thinking. When I offer drawing as an intervention, it may be that the client has said something that sounds like an image that could be made visual. For example, one widow said her grief felt like a whirlpool that was sucking her in. Inviting her to draw this image, I then asked her to visualize what or who could keep her from drowning. We talked about what could help her and she drew this into the picture as we discussed it. She felt relief when the drawing was completed.

Another client talked about a dark cloud over her head that seemed to follow her around. She readily accepted a large piece of paper and a box of oil pastels to demonstrate what she was feeling. She chose a dark grey crayon and quickly filled the page with a childlike representation of a cloud. When her cloud was finished, I asked her to imagine what was behind it. She drew a sun peeking out and shining down on her. She identified this sun as her deceased father, and even though her drawing was as primitive as a child's, she smiled and felt better after completing it.

Observing their creative expression after they have completed it enables clients to potentially shift how they feel. Our own reflection can offer guidance towards that possibility, yet often, clients themselves will discover insight and even comfort through the use of non-verbal modalities. I do not comment on their process until after they have shared what it means to them and what it evokes.

When a person is feeling very emotional, drawing what is happening inside helps them visualize it and move it out of their bodies. They can then engage with their drawing and connect it to their inner experience. This can be in the form of an energy drawing. Clients are invited to close their eyes, sense the emotions, or simply feel the energy within the body. Tuning in to that sensation and choosing a color to represent it, clients can draw its shape on the page. Drawing out anxiety, fear, panic, or sadness releases some of it on to the page. Using non-verbal modalities of color, line, and shape opens up a different avenue for processing these emotions.

MUSIC AND MOVEMENT

Music connects us organically with emotion. Many of my clients speak of their response to a particular song that randomly plays on their car radio, seeming to be a message from their significant person. Some may avoid music because it makes them cry, but they also find that music connects them to their love, their relationship, and to themselves.

Music that touches on the experience of grief or that reminds clients of their significant person can be played in the counseling office and clients can express what is meaningful or how they are moved by this music. They might create a playlist of meaningful songs and we would then listen to one or two in the office, after which they can tell the story of how it relates to their significant person or why they are so moved by it. Sometimes I play a specific song for a client because I believe it will be helpful for them. Gentle, soothing music played in the background during a session can contribute to a feeling of safety and calm in the environment.

Movement is another way to release emotion. Dancing in the privacy of your home to meaningful music expresses feeling and also serves to release pent-up energy. Since my late husband and I loved to dance, I would sometimes put on music that reminded me of him and imagine him dancing with me as I closed my eyes, remembering how we enjoyed that. This might make me weep, but it also made me smile warmly as I imagined he was dancing with me.

When clients are tense with emotion, I ask them to move their body to release it. We might stand together and shake it out, or I may suggest gentle swaying to generate more flow. One client came in filled with anger which he was having trouble containing. We stood facing each other, holding our hands in front of us, and I asked him to make tight fists, hold this pose for a beat, and then release his arms on a breath. We did this several times and this exercise gave him a way to grab his anger tight and then release it. He said he realized he did not have to hold on to it, and nor did he need to react to his rage that was leading him to a feeling of wanting to hit someone. He realized he could go off by himself for a few minutes when he was angry and do this clenching and release that effectively discharged his anger before having to deal with the person who was stimulating his anger.

IMAGERY

Engaging with visual imagery stimulates the right side of the brain, the location of creativity. This creative center responds in a more intuitive, reflective way, which then informs the more ratiocinated verbal side of the brain. Using imagery to stimulate the imagination in turn fosters storytelling as the client reflects on what arises in response to the image.

The type of imagery available for this purpose is infinite. You could gather photographs of scenery, boats sailing on the ocean, forests, sheep grazing on a hillside, or cityscapes. Ask the client to choose one or two pictures and then to respond to them. They may be invited to tell a story that relates to how they feel about the pictures or what they remind them of relating to the person who has died.

If they wish, they can bring in photographs from their relationship that can then be used for sharing memories. A widowed person might bring in wedding photographs or photographs from a special vacation they took that will enable them to tell stories. This is also a good technique to use with those whose loss happened a long time ago, as in the case of the death of a parent when the client was young. Later in life, particularly at transitional times, an adult who lost a parent as a child will express longing for the relationship they never had, even questioning whether they were truly loved by this person. Photographs can provide a springboard for this kind of discussion, in which they might notice how that parent is gazing at them or how they are being held. They can then begin to create a narrative that heals this longing.

I often use decks of cards with images on them, asking my client to choose three, observe and absorb what they see, and then share how they are affected by the images they chose. Deborah Koff-Chapin's beautiful *Soul Cards* are evocative and colorful and do not contain any meaning other than what the person gazing at them sees. There are several decks of *Soul Cards*, and I find them effective for this purpose. Deborah has also gathered her images into a series of coloring books, and a client might enjoy coloring the images and then responding to them by writing about the experience on the back. I have listed them in the Resources section at the end of the book.

There has been a surge in coloring books for adults to use for calming and enjoyment. While I do not use coloring books in my office, I do recommend them to clients who are having trouble regulating emotions in between sessions and who are looking for techniques to soothe themselves. There are coloring books of mandalas, flowers, fractals, and other images. Deborah Koff-Chapin has five coloring books of her touch drawings in black and white. These are organized in themes such as Gifts of the Feminine and Creative Awakening. More information about these can be found in the Resources section.

Guided imagery is another way for grieving people to access their inner experience of loss. Through this process, they may imagine that they are meeting their loved one and have a conversation with them. Or they might be guided to see themselves in a beautiful place, washed over with a sense of peace and calm. This can help them when their emotions are highly aroused. You could develop a script to use for guided meditation or spontaneously create one in the moment. You can also find ideas for guided meditation online, and these are included on some of the websites and publications of Alexandra Kennedy and Heather Stang (please see the Resources section for more information).

REFRAMING

When a client's narrative seems stuck or they repeat a phrase that expresses an inability to move through their grief, the first approach is to encourage them to tell that part of their story. Grief can feel stagnant and a person may feel frozen in time, as if nothing will ever be right in their lives again. Allow them to fully express this feeling rather than contradicting them or attempting to move them too quickly out of this stuck place. Afterwards, they could be invited to change the repeated phrase, to investigate whether there may be a different way of viewing their situation. What feels frozen may not actually be solid. When they are ready, they might be able to look at their story through a different lens. This, too, is creative process in action.

Cognitive behavioral therapy (CBT) techniques of replacing a statement with a different one are effective for some grievers. Some feelings are so overwhelming that the griever cannot see how they will ever feel differently. Definitive sounding comments that use words like "never" or "cannot" or express a certainty that their sorrow and distress will never end can be validated in the moment since they are expressing how they feel. Later, you could inquire if there may be a different way of stating their experience, perhaps recognizing that they are not the feeling—rather, it is something they are having in that moment.

Metaphors are also a creative way to help a client reframe how they feel. If their statement contains one, the metaphor becomes the vehicle for a shift in perspective through deepening the image by using story. A client who comments on their habit of stuffing their emotions can be asked to consider other things in their life that are stuffed away. Does this habit of avoidance serve a purpose? Is it protective or does pushing emotion down prevent the client from coping with the feelings? This consideration can lead to a discussion of actual objects that are stuffed, such as pillows and comforters, which can then be metaphorically used to cushion the feelings, wrapping the client up in a cozy way until they are ready to allow themself to engage with and process them.

Chapter 4

GRIEF MODELS

THE SHATTERING OF THE ASSUMPTIVE WORLD

Long before Elisabeth Kübler-Ross began working with dying patients and their families, psychologists and psychiatrists were investigating the cognitive, emotional, physical, and mental impacts of grief. Some of this work came out of returning soldiers after World War I, many of whom exhibited serious mental distress from spending months in muddy trenches bombarded with explosions, poison gas, and often having to share those claustrophobic, filthy spaces with dead comrades. I have already mentioned the work of Erich Lindemann with survivors affected by the tragedy at the Cocoanut Grove nightclub fire. In England, psychiatrist Colin Murray Parkes began treating widows in his hospital and wondered whether it was their grief that was a contributing factor to their psychiatric problems. He collaborated with another psychiatrist, Dr John Bowlby, who had been researching attachment by studying mothers and babies. Together they applied attachment theory to bereavement, demonstrating that the type of attachment style you have from childhood can influence later relationships (Bowlby 1977; Bowlby and Parkes 1970; Parkes 1987). The relationship and the type of attachment you have to a significant person who subsequently dies also strongly influences how you approach grief and creates conditions that either support resilience or cause complications.

Parkes and Bowlby observed that the death of a spouse or other significant person severely affected how the griever perceived their life and how they expected it to unfold. The distress felt about how everything had changed was hard for the bereaved person to manage since everything that they had assumed about their lives was gone. Parkes and Bowlby framed this impact by saying that grief shatters the assumptive world (Bowlby 1977; Bowlby and Parkes 1970; Parkes 1987).

We tend to think of our lives as linear trajectories in which we grow, develop friendships and relationships, start careers and families, purchase homes, and learn new things. If our lives are relatively comfortable, we assume that our plans will come to fruition. We assume things about how our lives will unfold. We project ourselves into a future and imagine how it will be.

Of course, life generally does not follow a prescribed plan but usually, if we lose a job or get divorced or relocate to a different home or city, we don't feel shattered by this change; if we do, we are able to move through those emotions with relative ease.

And some deaths are also like that—a beloved family member who dies at nearly 100 is mourned differently than a spouse who dies at age 37, leaving a widow with small children to raise alone. Family members of a person who dies after a lifelong struggle with mental illness and addiction may feel quite sad that their life was so difficult, but also relief that their struggle is over. Another family in a similar situation might experience anger at the person who died and then feel guilty about this anger.

For others, especially those whose loved one was young or the breadwinner of the family or the sole emotional supporter, the world can seem very broken. The griever can feel lost. This impacts a person's sense of identity but also affects the realm of those world assumptions that we live by, almost unconsciously. Habits, ways of participating in our social world, all aspects of life seem to require re-evaluation. Before the death, the griever expected a certain amount of permanence and believed that they were in control of their lives. Now, who they are and how they operate in their own world needs adjustment. Dr Sameet Kumar, a psychologist who works with terminally ill patients and their families, points out that humans tend to project themselves into the future and believe in that "future self" as something real:

> One of the reasons grief can feel so disorienting is that when your loved one dies or leaves, this future self becomes unraveled; all the plans you made together are now impossible. As days pass—days you had hoped to share with your loved one—your loneliness may be all the more apparent. (Kumar 2005, p.92)

The fact is, we begin constructing our model of how the world works from childhood and everything we experience, who we relate to, our experiences, even how we think of ourselves—all these influence the assumptions we create. Most of the time, our model and assumptions are proved to be valid and we are comfortable in our lives and believe that we are in control of it. When our assumptions are challenged, the world view we relied upon falters. Some of these challenges play out in positive ways; we may be exposed to new things such as traveling to different countries and experiencing different cultures from which we can learn to think differently, assume differently, and develop new perceptions about how the world works. In a comfortable, well-ordered world, our behaviors and our relationships tend to become automatic. Things feel stable and we assume they will remain so. When death challenges who we are, how we relate, and how we function in the world, our reliance on this stability is also shattered. This can cause anxiety, making the world feel unsafe. Add to this typical grief symptoms of brain fog, fear, and lack of concentration, and the griever has difficulty making sense of how their world has changed:

> The familiar world suddenly seems to have become unfamiliar, habits of thought can let us down, we have lost confidence in our most essential possession, our internal model of the world, and because of this we may lose confidence in ourselves. (Parkes and Prigerson 2010, p.103)

Not every bereaved person will feel that their world is shattered. Others might experience the distress of changing roles and assumptions for a short time, some for longer. As a griever moves through the different aspects of their loss, uncovering how their life has changed and slowly moving towards figuring out how they want to live after loss, it is possible to construct new assumptions, new habits of thought more aligned to the world as it is now. The challenge of rebuilding, or even of relearning the world, as phenomenologist Thomas Attig puts it (2011), may seem a daunting one in the early part of grief. It is hard to know what the future will look like, and in the midst of aroused emotions, along with the longing and loneliness that often accompany loss, the shape of the world is difficult to imagine. As the person moves through the pain and sorrow, slowly they will begin to discover how they might want their world to look, feel, and to be. They begin to reconstruct themselves and their world.

There are some circumstances of death that are extremely challenging. While I believe in the possibility of growth and even transformation after tragedy, when someone has lost a child they are probably not interested in talking about transformation. Multiple losses due to accidents when several family members are killed or natural disasters are often so life-shattering that the grieving person cannot think about growth for a long time. How could such horror be a lesson? This is also the case, as we are seeing more often, in random mass shootings or with hate crimes, although some people are galvanized to channel their grief into activism. It is important to understand, though, that advocacy does not replace grief. People affected by these terrible tragedies still need support to feel their pain and to express it, without judgment of any kind.

Suicide is another type of death that carries with it many complex reactions. There is often a sense of betrayal and a questioning of the relationship itself. Survivors of suicide are often quite angry at their loved one for not considering those who would be left behind to clean up their mess, figuratively and sometimes literally. While mental illness, depression, and despair are almost always the cause of suicide, the grieving survivor fluctuates between understanding that underlying condition and their own emotions. In addition, the suicide survivor is often questioned by unknowing and insensitive outsiders, asking why they were not able to stop the death, or if they were aware of the possibility of suicide. The survivor is already ruminating on these questions themselves, but when they come from other people, they seem judgmental and shift the responsibility of the death from the person who completed suicide to the survivor.[1]

Some survivors of suicide spend many years attempting to help their loved one with their depression, PTSD, or other diagnosed mental illness only to be unsuccessful. Others are blindsided by the suicide as the person who died effectively hid their despair as well as their plan to take their own life. The survivor is left with many questions as they attempt

---

1   When someone kills themselves, it is common to say that they "committed" suicide. This word seems to imply that suicide is a crime. In an attempt to lessen the societal stigma surrounding suicide, survivors of suicide as well, as many therapists who work with families affected by suicide, prefer the term "completed suicide."

to parse out the reasons, along with all the other emotional, physical, and psychological reactions to the death. The counseling office can be a safe space for them to articulate these questions and to say out loud what they are unable to say to the person who died, and to those who are judging or seeking to blame someone else for the suicide.

KÜBLER-ROSS'S FIVE STAGES

Elisabeth Kübler-Ross was a Swiss medical student who emigrated to the USA where she continued to train to be a psychiatrist. During her residency, she worked with terminally ill patients and was shocked at their treatment by the medical profession. She wondered if these patients knew how ill they were, and was puzzled by the doctors who refused to address the facts about their condition with the patients and with their families.

It was common practice in the early 1960s for doctors and family members to withhold information about disease prognosis from patients. Kübler-Ross believed that this caused undue distress in these patients, especially when they were aware of their own deteriorating condition, and in most cases, could intuit that they were indeed dying. She felt that dying people deserved to have a voice, so she began speaking with them to find out how they felt and what they knew. She discovered that in many cases, they were grateful for the opportunity to speak about it and were grateful to finally have someone who was willing to listen to how they felt. She began using these conversations as a teaching tool in seminars for psychiatry and medical students.

Kübler-Ross observed some common themes in what these patients expressed. Her first book, *On Death and Dying*, was published in 1969 and identified five commonalities that terminally ill patients coped with, with their impending death. One important factor in her work is that she never expected these common themes, which she referred to as stages, to become a model for every person who is dying. Kübler-Ross did not identify these stages as a linear path that must be followed. She states clearly that some people only felt one of these stages, while some felt two or three. These stages were not meant to be in any particular order; rather, Kübler-Ross noted that the 200 or so patients she spoke with coped in some of these ways. She even has a disclaimer in this book, saying that these are not meant to be taken as a straight-line model.

Her subsequent book, *On Grief and Grieving*, was written with her associate David Kessler as Kübler-Ross herself was dying (see the Resources section at the end of the book). She did not live to see its completion. In this book, Kübler-Ross and Kessler applied these five "stages" to bereavement. They also referred to the stages as defense mechanisms. Again, they clearly state that it is not necessary to "complete" all five or even any of these stages, as they were never meant to be a definitive method for coping with grief.

The stages have evolved since their introduction, and have been very misunderstood over the past three decades. They were never meant to help such messy emotions into neat packages. They are responses to loss that many people have, but there is not a typical response to loss, as there is no typical loss. Our grief is as individual as our lives. (Kübler-Ross and Kessler 2005, p.7)

While many people do experience variations of anger, denial, bargaining, depression, and acceptance, a grieving person might experience two or even more of these "stages" at once, or go back and forth between different them or even skip some of them. The thanatology community generally objects to the word "stages" because they seem too passive; they might be better understood as "states" rather than "stages." In fact, Kessler now refers to them as "areas" of grief rather than stages.

In my opinion there are three problems with the five stages of grief:

- One, every grieving person is unique, and so the way they grieve will be subtly different from another person. When helping a grieving client, it is important to understand their family history, how they are used to expressing emotion, their culture, the type of relationship, as well as the type of event that caused them to grieve.

- Two, using this model as it has been popularly misunderstood leads to the concept that there is a right way to grieve, which means there must be a wrong way. Many doctors, nurses, and healthcare professionals as well as uninformed lay people have the erroneous idea that if the grieving person can move through five steps in a certain amount of time, their grief will be over and done with. This view then leads to judgment on the part of professionals that there is not only a right way to grieve but also a finite amount of time in which to conclude this grief. The idea that grief must be completed in stages and within a certain amount of time dismisses the internal experience of the bereaved person and can lead to incorrect labels of psychological disorders when, in fact, grief takes longer than most people can accept.

- Three, this model is 50 years old. There has been a large body of research done on bereavement and how we grieve since then, and many of these models are more flexible, more useful, and contain a more cogent view of grief in modern times.

While many people will experience one or more of these identified states, we don't have to apply this model (or any one way of working through grief, for that matter) as if it is *the best and only way*. The question is, how will our clients cope with their reactions to any of these states if they do arise?

Denial

Kübler-Ross identified denial as the first stage. In *On Death and Dying* (Kübler-Ross 1969, p.51) she calls this stage "Denial and Isolation," and says that terminally ill patients have difficulty believing that the diagnosis is true. Patients, often wisely, seek second or third opinions or alternative treatments. This is similar to a condition of shock that often exists in early grief. A common refrain I hear from my bereaved clients in the first few months after a death is this: "I can't believe she is gone." While this sounds like denial, it is actually part of the long process of adjustment that leads to acceptance. Statements like these are not a denial of the event; rather, the person is expressing that at the moment, it is too much to bear or to integrate.

I am not particularly fond of the word "denial" because it seems dismissive. People on the outside have been heard to say, "He's in denial," which implies that the griever should just get a grip on reality. Instead, I witness again and again that to accept the radical change that death can create in a person's life takes time. The shock and sorrow fluctuate with awareness of these changes. The back and forth between disbelief and figuring out how to cope with death continues for a quite a while, usually much longer than the griever is comfortable with. It certainly continues longer than corporations or some medical professionals expect. In my opinion, we need to be very careful to recognize that each person's grief will take a unique amount of time and not hurry them with words suggesting that they are too slow to process their reactions to grief. There is enough pressure from the outside world with misguided suggestions to just buck up and get on with life. The grieving client does not need to encounter this from the person they have come to for help.

Questions such as "Are they really dead?" or "How did this happen?" or "Why me?" are common in early grief. These help the reality trickle in, which is a process that requires exploration. It is our job as practitioners to allow for this time, and to encourage our clients to take it.

It is important to allow our clients to feel and then explore their sense of shock and disbelief. It is important for them to be given time to learn how to live again. For some people this can take between six months and a year, but for most, the extreme fluctuations of grief can take one to three years before the person begins to feel regulated and comfortable in their new life.

Anger

Many people feel angry when someone dies. This may be related to the circumstances of the death or to the age of the person. Anger may arise when the death is sudden or the changes in the bereaved person's life seem to be radical now that this person is gone. Some people feel angry at the doctors who diagnosed the disease—perhaps if they had "caught" the disease sooner the person would have been able to survive. I have witnessed this angry response even when a person was terminally ill for many years.

Anger is one of the strongest and often loudest emotions. In some people, it bursts out like a flame thrower, strafing everyone in its path. In others, it is a slow, simmering burn. If it is not released in some way, it can sear a person from the inside. Therefore, a good way to process anger is from the inside out.

Anger has a purpose. Allow your client to express their anger, explore it, and see what is behind it. Often, anger is a protective mechanism because the pain inside is too hard to hold:

> If we ask people to move through their anger too fast, we only alienate them. Whenever we ask people to be different than they are, or to feel something different, we are not accepting them as they are and where they are. Nobody likes to be asked to change and not be accepted as they are. We like it even less in the midst of grief. (Kübler-Ross and Kessler 2005, p.14)

Bargaining

This stage is definitely more prevalent in terminal illness and does not show up as much after the death. There is really nothing to bargain with once the person is gone, so I don't feel that bargaining is particularly present in bereavement.

There is, however, often a period in which the person questions whether there was anything that could have been done that would possibly have changed the outcome. Perhaps a third opinion would have offered a new treatment that would have cured the cancer? A grieving person might state, "If only I had convinced him not to drive in that thunderstorm," taking on the responsibility for an accident. Guilty feelings and "If only..." questions do arise. Kessler and Kübler-Ross include these in their bereavement bargaining stage.

Depression

The emotions of grief are hard to manage. If a widow or widower has been married a long time, learning to live without a partner they spent the majority of their lives with is very hard. When an adult loses a parent they considered a best friend, they have lost an ally, a regular conversation partner, and a supporter. And in the case of child loss, parents reel from the shock of such a terrible injustice for a long time. These situations are terribly dark and the bereaved person has trouble seeing any hope of a real life after this death.

This looks and feels like depression. Grievers have trouble getting out of bed or completing normal tasks. Concentration is affected by grief and some people feel as if they are floating slowly through the world or walking through mud. This also sounds like depression.

Grief leaves many people feeling empty and without a sense of purpose. They may have trouble imagining how they will live without this important person. Yet, this depressive reaction is generally different than classic clinical depression that often has no discernable causality. It is important to be aware of this when working with a grieving person, to validate their depressive feelings as normal as well as to be aware of any previous underlying depressive tendencies that may have existed before the death. Knowing the client's psychological history will help you parse this out, and it is wise to periodically check in with the client to notice the difference. In cases where your client has had a history of clinical depression, be mindful that grief can stimulate this prior history.

Grief-related depression is not something to be fixed, but we can help our clients manage these feelings as well as encourage them to allow them to arise. Remember, life has changed radically for the client and they need to engage with all the emotions in order to move through them. Kübler-Ross suggests viewing depression as a slightly unwelcome guest:

> Invite your depression to pull up a chair with you in front of the fire, and sit with it, without looking for a way to escape. Allow the sadness and emptiness to cleanse you and help you explore your loss in its entirety. When you allow yourself to experience depression, it will leave as soon as it has served its purpose in your loss. As you grow stronger, it may return from time to time, but that is how grief works. (Kübler-Ross and Kessler 2005, p.22)

Acceptance

Accepting a death is a long and tricky process with many parts. One part is accepting that life has changed now that this person is no longer alive. The type of relationship, the type of death, and how a person's life is therefore affected by this fact will influence how the griever comes to terms with the death and its impact. In spousal loss, there are so many issues surrounding the death of a partner. A widow now has to assume the daily tasks that her partner took care of. She might have suddenly become a single parent and has to juggle twice as much since she no longer has the partner's help. Perhaps an elderly widower never had to cook for himself or write a check, and now he has to figure out where the bank is and how to feed himself healthy food.

Another problem for widowed people is the loss of physical closeness and intimacy. Some widowed people develop what is called "skin hunger," a physical longing for touch. There is often a dilemma about which side of the bed to sleep on, whether or not to change the decor in the bedroom or elsewhere in the home. Reminders are everywhere, and it is both hard to see them and difficult to remove them. How long should the clothes of the deceased remain in the closet? How does the griever feel about photographs, setting the table for one less person, or doing all the driving when the other partner was the one who usually drove?

As practitioners whose focus should be on allowing the bereaved person to figure out what is right for them, we should be very careful not to apply any particular timeline to any of these issues. There is a wide spectrum of time in which people feel able to deal with the belongings of their dead spouse. There are people who immediately divest of clothes and personal items, but most people wait. Some wait a year or more. Please be sensitive to what feels right for your client and recognize that it is different for each person. And sometimes a person may state that they are ready and then discover that they are actually not.

It is very likely that a parent will never accept the death of a child and a widowed person might always have some trouble fully integrating the changes in their life after a spouse dies. People who are widowed early feel cheated by not being able to grow old with their partner as they expected. People whose marriage lasted 30, 60, or 70 years have difficulty coping with being alone as they may not have lived alone, ever. Complete acceptance of an event implies that one's emotional reaction to it is over and done with. In many cases, a bereaved person is never finished with grief because it will rear up again, triggered by new events where that person is missing. New losses can also trigger grief reactions relating to prior ones. But if acceptance means learning to be comfortable in your own life after a significant person is no longer in it, then acceptance can be achieved.

I hope you have received the message that these five stages, while felt by many bereaved people, do not represent a simple, five-step method to "get over" grief. Grief is a lifelong process, and it takes time to integrate loss into your life and learn how to live with it.

WORDEN'S TASKS OF MOURNING

William Worden is a psychologist, grief therapist, and thanatologist, and has been lecturing in the field since the 1982. His work is based on attachment theory, referencing the seminal work of John Bowlby. He also makes a semantic distinction between the terms *grief*, *mourning* and *bereavement*. Worden uses the word grief to mean the experience of the person who has lost someone. To him, the word *mourning* refers to the "*process* that one goes through in *adapting* to the death of the person." Worden continues, defining bereavement as "the loss to which the person is trying to adapt and the experience of having lost someone close" (Worden 2018, p.18).

To me, the words grief and bereavement are interchangeable and refer to the experience of loss. Mourning defines the activities and rituals people engage with during the grieving process. Wherever you fall in this semantical debate, it is generally considered that mourning is somewhat different than grief or bereavement.

Worden's model is called the tasks of mourning. He believes that stages indicate a passive activity while tasks are something you can do. In his first edition of *Grief Counseling and Grief Therapy: A Handbook for the Mental Health Practitioner*, published in 1982, he included three tasks, which were to accept the reality of the loss, to experience the pain, and to adjust to life afterwards. His fourth task was to withdraw emotional energy away from the deceased. This was in keeping with the concept that was promulgated by Freud, Kübler-Ross, and even Worden, that once acceptance of the loss has been reached and the emotionality of the reaction has been dealt with, a person can adjust and get on with their lives. Lindemann said that after a year or so, a grieving person would probably get back to normal.

We now understand that this is unrealistic. When someone significant is gone from your life, their influence continues, in a positive, negative, or ambivalent way depending on the type of relationship. In fact, many bereaved people long to continue a sense of connection in some form with their loved ones. Even in cases where the dead person was abusive or the relationship was problematic, threads of connection still exist as the griever copes with the aftermath and works towards healing. Thanatologists call the activity of having some kind of relationship with the deceased "continuing bonds." Worden, responding to the thanatological research of others and in his own practice experience, understood this, and subsequent editions of his book include a fourth task, to continue a relationship to the deceased in some form while the bereaved person reinvests in their own life. Worden says:

> In both the second and third editions of this book, I suggested that the fourth task of mourning is to find a place for the deceased but in a way that will not preclude him or her from going on with life. We need to find ways to memorialize, that is, to remember dead loved ones—keeping them with us but still going on with life. In this edition, I have rewritten the fourth task as follows: to find an enduring connection with the deceased in the midst of embarking on a new life. (Worden 2009, p.50)

In his Fifth edition, Worden revises his fourth task to carry the memory of the deceased person through the rest of one's life, not just in the process of reengaging in living soon after the death (Worden 2018 p.51).

Worden's first task is to accept the reality of the loss. He noted that in early grief, the bereaved person must accept that the person is never coming back, even as they yearn and pine for their return. Worden stated:

> Coming to acceptance of the reality of the loss takes time since it involves not only an intellectual acceptance but also an emotional one. Many less experienced counselors do not recognize this and focus too much on mere intellectual acceptance of the loss, overlooking emotional acceptance. The bereaved person may be intellectually aware of the finality of the loss long before the emotions allow full acceptance of the information as true. (Worden 2009, p.42)

Since releasing his 2018 fifth edition of *Grief Counseling and Grief Therapy*, Worden has broadened his first task. He stated in a lecture in April 2019 that he now includes a broader view of acceptance that includes acknowledgement of the loss. This reflects an understanding that acceptance is a multi-leveled process, and that most people do not need a reality check as much as they need time to acknowledge the impact of the death on their lives.

It is as if there are two ways of knowing. The person knows intellectually that the person they are grieving is actually dead. Yet this knowledge exists only in the mind and has not actually been completely absorbed in all realms. The person may have moments when they forget and call their loved one to come down for dinner. Or they might dream that they are alive and well. I think there is a dichotomy between intellectual knowing and a more visceral awareness that settles into our body, our cellular structure, our felt sense. I see it as the reality of the loss slowly dripping in to all the areas of a person's life.

This dichotomy is common among all grievers, even if they are caring for a person who is dying. Family members of a terminally ill patient and those who have been long-term caregivers often say that they believe that during the dying process they are preparing for the death. Some think that this period of anticipatory grief will eliminate the need to grieve once the death takes place. To their surprise, they are often blindsided by the shock they feel. It does seem, though, that shock and disbelief do not last as long with those who had been aware that the person was going to die and who also engaged in some anticipatory mourning. For those who experience a sudden unexpected death, shock and disbelief last much longer, as does the task of accepting the reality of the loss.

Worden wisely stresses the importance of experiencing all of the emotions that arise, recognizing that attempts to bury feelings or avoid them will ultimately be detrimental, and even impossible. His second task calls for processing this pain, because "[i]t is necessary to acknowledge and work through this pain or it can manifest itself through physical symptoms or some form of aberrant behavior" (Worden 2009, p.44).

As practitioners, it is imperative that we accept any and all emotional expressions of grief (except those that might physically harm the bereaved person or another) and help our clients process them. So many people think that suppressing "negative" emotions is better, and some people have even been trained from a young age not to express anger, fear, or distress because it might disturb others. Bereaved people worry about being a burden if their emotions become too large and loud, or they fear that if they give in to these feelings, they will never be able to stop crying or they will completely fall apart. They need support, safety, and encouragement to explore the "darker" aspects of their feelings so that they can be moved through and somewhat released. Holding them inside can lead to illness or random outbursts in inappropriate places.

Worden mentions that not everyone experiences grief in such an intense way, although the majority of people will experience some pain after the loss of someone important to them. He also highlights how societal norms and expectations can interfere with the task of processing pain and other emotions. The griever may be subjected to messages that dismiss the depth of their reactions, suggesting that they are indulging in a "pity party" or they would feel better if they could "just be strong." One of the tasks of a practitioner helping a grieving person is to encourage them to engage with the pain of grief in order to move through it. Often the "should" statements come from the grievers themselves as they question whether they are "doing this right." This is an opportunity for us to help them explore how they work with their own grief and offer them support in their process.

Worden's third task has to do with adjusting to the world after the loss, which Worden divides into three areas: the external, which is about everyday functioning; the internal, which is about a person's sense of self; and the spiritual, which is how "death affects one's beliefs, values, and assumptions about the world" (Worden 2009, p.46).

It is difficult to adjust to a world without someone who is integral to it. This can be true even if the relationship is a difficult one; there is a pattern to a relationship and often there are different roles, whether these are concretely or more subtly defined. Worden points out:

> The survivor usually is not aware of all the roles played by the deceased until sometime after the loss occurs. (Worden 2018, p.47)

When a parent dies, the surviving adult child may be struck with the realization of how much they relied on this parent for advice and companionship. Or if the adult child was an active caregiver, they may feel as if they have lost a "job" and certainly, they have lost a focus, as many carers maintain a level of vigilant attention towards an ailing relative. External adjustments also include taking on responsibilities that were once shared or feeling the loss of being the person who offered guidance and comfort if it is a child who has died.

Internal adjustments need to be made as the bereaved struggle with changes in their sense of self. Grief can feel like an identity crisis (covered more fully in Chapter 5, under "W" of the "WHOLE process"). Worden discussed how these changes affect individuals as they question who they are, perhaps even suffering damage to how they feel about themselves. Worden says, "Bereavement can also affect a person's sense of *self-efficacy*—the degree to which people feel that they have some control over what happens to them" (Worden 2009, p.48; original emphasis). Our job as counselors is to help grievers explore who they are now, to rediscover their inner strengths and resiliencies that will help them make these adjustments. For activities to help with this, see Part Two of this book.

Spiritual adjustments, as defined by Worden, include religious, spiritual, or philosophical beliefs. Some devout people observe that they do not find solace in their house of worship the way they used to, or they even stop attending for a time. Others may seek out spirituality in a way that they did not before the death. And grievers often feel unmoored in their own lives, as if how they perceived it and how they expected it to be has been shattered as well the assumptions they have created.

Worden changed his fourth task after recognizing that putting the relationship in the past in order to move on is usually not possible. His fourth task is to learn to discover ways to continue a relationship with the deceased while re-engaging in life. Continuing bonds can be accomplished in many ways, including the use of memories, physical reminders, and recognizing what you have learned from the deceased that will be useful going forward.

Worden objects to Elisabeth Kübler-Ross's stages, feeling that they were too passive and linear. To him, a stage is something that happens to you, but a task is something you engage with. Worden also understands that grief is not simplistic and offers mediators of each task, based on attachment theory. These mediators clarify some of the unique reactions to grief, as we are affected by the type of relationship, the cause of death, the time of death, and the age of the person, including our own age. Grief expressions relate to cultural norms and family patterns of coping with loss, trauma, and emotion. Societal expectations, self-esteem, willingness to engage with emotions or to bottle them up, all these various tendencies modify how a person responds to death.

For example, a widow who was married for over 60 years loses her husband over a long decline of about two years. She cared for him and witnessed his cognitive and physical deterioration until he finally died. This is a fairly common story, but each widow, experiencing this scenario, will react differently. One widow might feel completely lost within her life and fear that she will not be able to take care of daily tasks without her lifelong partner. She may weep often, and feel depressed and very lonely. This widow may worry that she is not coping well and fear that she will never again feel complete or whole. Another widow with the same circumstances may feel calm and celebrate the successful life of her lifelong love. This widow might express concern that she is not that sad, although she does miss her husband very much. Another widow, freed of the burden of intense and debilitating caregiving, may finally be able to engage in activities that were put on hold, finding new things to learn, and enjoying the experience of being single again. This does not dismiss the relationship or the shared love; rather, it represents the ability to continue to grow.

Sometimes an adult reacts very strongly to the death of a parent. This parent might have been seen as the most supportive person in their life, or even been considered a best friend. There may have been enmeshment in the relationship. Sometimes children have a difficult relationship with one parent and a close relationship with the other, which can cause some issues when the close parent dies. Other people, while resolved to the death of a parent after a long drawn-out illness, still find a loss of meaning in their lives as they look back at their own choices and forwards towards their own mortality.

The unique quality of each person's grief is demonstrated by mediators of grief that relate to attachment theory. Worden's application of these offers a deeper view of how a person approaches their tasks and how they might accomplish them. When viewed through the lens of attachment, you may be able to understand tendencies that make each griever different from someone else. It might be more difficult for a person with an ambivalent attachment to their dead parent to continue the connection; they may not even want to, which would be appropriate for them. A person with a more avoidant or dissociative attachment style may have a harder time tapping into their own emotions, while a person with a more secure style might dive into emotional expression readily. A griever who feels they had a good relationship with the deceased might have an easier time adjusting to life after the death if they are more secure in their relationships with others.

The type of relationship, the circumstances of the death, the age of the person who died, historical, cultural and societal norms, these all subtly change how a person will grieve.

Worden offers seven mediators of grief:

- *Kinship:* Who was the person who died and what kind of relationship did the bereaved person have with them? The depth and duration of the grieving process often depends on this; an elderly relative who lived a full life might be missed but may not generate acute grief. The death of a child, however, will most likely cause intense emotional reactions, confusion, and extended periods of questioning and longing. Spousal loss impacts the surviving spouse in many ways, not only the loss of the partner and intimacy, but this will often also have practical impacts.

- *Attachment:* Was the attachment strong, secure, ambivalent, conflicted, or dependent? Worden says, "It is almost axiomatic that the intensity of grief is determined by the intensity of love. The grief reaction often increases in severity proportionately to the intensity of the love relationship" (2018, p.60).

- *Circumstances of the death:* How the person died affects how someone grieves. Was the death natural? Was it sudden, or did it come after a prolonged illness? Was there an accident, suicide, or homicide? How old was the person when they died? Was the bereaved present at the time of death or far away? Finally, there are circumstances of multiple deaths that strongly affect how survivors respond. All these circumstances mediate the tasks that Worden proposes.

- *Personal history:* How has the bereaved coped with prior losses? Are there any underlying mental health issues that may interfere with how they cope with and process grief? What is their family history of approaching emotion, change, and loss? Were there losses from long ago that feel unresolved?

- *Personality:* Aspects of personality also influence how a person will move through grief. Attachment and coping styles, optimistic or pessimistic outlooks, self-esteem, and values and beliefs all affect the process of bereavement.

- *Societal influences:* The level of support a grieving person has in their social context greatly affects how they will process grief. Humans are social, relational beings, and a person experiencing a difficult emotional event is helped by having people who care around them. Someone who has no social support will have a harder time coping with the emotional aspects of grief.

- *Change and secondary stress:* Many things can change in a person's life when someone dies, and these changes can create additional stress on the bereaved. When the primary wage earner dies, the household suffers in the midst of their grief. A widow might have to sell the family home, move to a different location, or take a new job to support the family, which might leave any children with a different type of parental contact. The death of a significant person in the family can cause a cascade of small changes that overwhelm the griever.

I find that Worden's task model is applicable to most grievers, especially in early grief. It gives them a framework for their grief and can be used in that way, as long as it is not applied rigidly or with an expectation that each task must be "completed" in order for grief to be "resolved."

DR ALAN WOLFELT'S COMPANIONING MODEL OF BEREAVEMENT

Dr Alan Wolfelt is a grief counselor, lecturer, and prolific author who offers a companioning model of bereavement. He believes that the practitioner's job is to compassionately listen, to witness the client's story and their emotion, and to walk alongside the client as they discover their pathway through their own loss. Wolfelt points out that grief is not something to be "treated." He does not see those who come to him for counseling as "patients," which to him means people who have been passively suffering for a long time. I also do not refer to the people who come to my office as patients—I am not a medical practitioner and they are not ill. Are they suffering? Yes. Do I have ideas and strategies that might be helpful? Absolutely, I do. But I agree with Wolfelt's concept that sharing and being a companion in grief in a friendly, warm way is a kind and accessible approach.

Wolfelt offers a long list of what companioning in grief counseling means. Here are a few highlights:

- Companioning is about curiosity; it is not about expertise.

- Companioning is about learning from others; it is not about teaching them.

- Companioning is about walking alongside; it is not about leading.

- Companioning is about being present to another person's pain; it is not about taking away the pain.

- Companioning is about going to the wilderness of the soul with another human being; it is not about thinking you are responsible for finding a way out. (Wolfelt 2003, p.6)

Since no one can fix another person's problems or their sense of disorientation and loss after someone dies, simply being with them while they explore their own experience is a good technique. The practitioner is a compassionate witness, a sympathetic person who does not judge. We are free to offer ideas for them to experiment with, we are free to ask them to reframe some looping, ruminating thoughts, but it is better to wait until all aspects of their experience have been explored.

Wolfelt has a series of *Healing Your Grieving Heart* books that are directed towards different types of loss. Each book contains 100 ways to cope, with a "carpe diem" at the bottom of the page that is a small suggestion or activity. He offers *Healing A Spouse's Grieving Heart* or *Healing a Parent's Grieving Heart* and many more. These are practical guides that contain simple techniques and I often recommend the appropriate version to clients who find comfort in reading.

Wolfelt's books can be found at his Center for Loss & Life Transition website and also at bookstores. I recommend reading a few of these for more information on his companioning approach. See the Resources section at the end of the book.

THE DUAL PROCESS MODEL OF COPING WITH BEREAVEMENT

Margaret Stroebe and Henk Schut (2013) have been conducting research in bereavement for several decades. Their model, called the dual process, explains the tension between feeling and doing, between experiencing emotion and accomplishing the daily tasks of living. The model is helpful in normalizing the upheaval and turmoil of grief as well as in granting permission to let go of emotional reactions sometimes.

For many people, the emotions of grief are exhausting. At the same time, even as the person is overwhelmed by longing, sadness, fear, insecurity, or anger, there are still activities that need to be taken care of. The bereaved might need to go back to work several days after the funeral and in many cases is expected to perform as if nothing happened. There might be children to take care of, to take to sporting events or music or dance lessons, to prepare food for, to actually parent. For some, keeping busy is an antidote to emotion, enabling the person to feel somewhat normal when they take care of daily business.

The dual process model highlights the fluctuation between feeling and doing, and demonstrates how people move back and forth between the two ways of experiencing grief, many times during the course of a day. A bereaved person may wake up feeling crushed and sad, then force themselves to get out of bed to get ready for the day. They take care of what needs to be done, and head off to work. Engaging in their job allows them to put aside their grief for a while. Then someone says something or a memory arises and they again feel emotion wash over them. They go off to a private place for a while, have a little cry, and then go back to work. And back and forth it goes.

Stroebe and Schut call this "oscillation." They noted through their research that people move back and forth in various ways. They call the feeling mode the "loss orientation" and the doing mode the "restorative orientation." They recognize that no one is all loss or all restorative; rather, everyone seems to oscillate, although some people do tend to lean in one direction more than the other. People have different coping styles and some focus more intently on the loss, discovering ways to live again through that focus. In loss orientation, grievers spend time working through what they lost, how they have been affected in their sense of self, and who they are in the world. Others cope more through activities, trying new things, and even new relationships. The restoration-oriented person often deals with the effects of loss on career, social standing, loneliness, and getting things done. Of course, both of these aspects of grief need to be managed, and most people incorporate both of these coping styles to varying degrees.

In a similar vein, Ken Doka proposes four coping styles—there are "heart grievers" and "head grievers," and there are people who process their grief in combination, that is, "heart + head grievers" and those who are more oppositional and cope in a "head vs. heart" mode. Again, these are not finite but represent a continuum of coping mechanisms (Doka, 2016, p.76).

Doka and his colleague Terry Martin also organize these coping approaches into three grieving styles (Doka 2016). The intuitive griever is more aligned with the dual process loss orientation, approaching their grief experience through the emotional field. The instrumental griever is one who aligns with the restoration orientation of the dual process, and their focus is more on the doing aspects of life after loss. Doka includes a blended grieving style, recognizing that many people grieve in combination of loss and restoration, or feeling and doing.

I find the dual process beneficial when a client is having difficulty getting through the day and accomplishing things that need to get done. These clients lean towards loss orientation, or what Doka calls intuitive grievers. I recommend that they approach daily tasks in small ways, by making lists and checking items off. It may be that their list is very long and they feel overwhelmed and unable to complete basic tasks. By encouraging them to check off one or two items on the list and getting them to congratulate themselves for getting those things done, they begin to see that they can indeed get a few things done.

Other clients believe that keeping themselves very busy will help them move through grief. These are the instrumental grievers and sometimes they might actually be avoiding their emotions. As long as their activities are not preventing them from feeling when emotions arise, I encourage them to do what feels comfortable. But sometimes a client comes in to my office because they are finding their emotions, untended, are rising up at inopportune times. They may find themselves extremely angry at work or have difficulty sleeping. They need more help with regulating their emotions and may also need to be encouraged to take the time to experience their emotions, to allow them to arise fully so that they can be released in more effective ways.

When I explain the dual process or different coping styles to clients, they usually find these ways of viewing the grief process reassuring. They are already experiencing oscillation, sometimes to the point of whiplash, so having this example normalizes their experience.

SOMATIC INTERVENTIONS

The body is the first responder to what happens in our lives. When we were infants, we cried when we were hungry or sleepy; we let our caregivers know that we wanted to be picked up or that we needed to be changed. An infant's world is almost entirely sensory, and the nervous system, connected to the brain, has a wisdom of its own. If we are geared towards creating an assumptive world out of what we perceive, we begin to develop our ideas about how our world works through these perceptions, called "neuroception" in the brain science world.

Humans know things through the body. While children are more attuned to this sensory awareness, adults learn to turn off their neuroceptive abilities or often rationalize them away. If we tune in, we can sense danger and are aware of shifts in energy and mood among people we are interacting with. Much of this information is perceived within the body before we begin to think about it. Tension in the shoulders, queasiness in the stomach, and a sudden rush of icy cold in the chest—these physical reactions occur before we understand them and sometimes, dismiss them.

Grief carries a lot of physical symptoms along with the inevitable emotional and cognitive reactions. Some people report tightness in the chest and difficulty breathing. Sleep is affected, as is appetite—some people feel hollow and attempt to fill up this feeling by eating a lot. Others forget to eat. The emotional disturbances of grief also take a physical toll—crying a lot depletes hydration, while lack of sleep and adequate nutrition along with anguish and despair can suppress the immune system.

Helping a grieving client calm some of these symptoms through somatic interventions enables them to gain some control over what feels like an uncontrollable situation. Learning how to use breath, to notice where tension is held, and to move the body to release it reduces some of the physical symptoms of grieving.

As a former dancer and choreographer, it is easy for me to tune into body language and subtle gestural nuances. I might notice that a client is leaning forward, slightly hunched, as they tell the story of what occurred in the time between sessions. I might subtly mirror their posture so that I can sense where the tension is. Then I gently bring their attention to the posture, asking how it feels. I might ask them to deepen into the posture, perhaps closing in on themselves more before using their breath to open up and to gently sit up straight, all the while noticing how the small shift in posture can also modify how they feel.

Another way to work somatically is to ask an emotional or activated client to close their eyes, feet flat on the floor, hands on knees. I ask them to take a deep, slow breath in, and to release it on a slightly longer exhale than the in-breath. I breathe along with them for three or four times. I might ask them to place a hand on their belly and one on their heart while they are breathing, in and out. This has a calming, grounding effect.

Noticing what is happening physically while your client is in your office is important and can provide clues that can be worked with. It is important to be sensitive and attuned to the client before you engage with them physically because sometimes opening the chest or lifting the heart can open the floodgates. Be prepared for any reaction and be prepared to help the client ground if that is what they need. Remember that a release of strong emotion that has been held tightly could be healthy, so it is wise to also allow for the flood to spill out for a while before helping them calm down.

The observation of physical cues in the client will enable you to perceive what may be happening within the tone of their emotions. Dr Robert Neimeyer, renowned grief therapist and researcher, suggests paying attention to the "affect trail" in order to be aware of the subtle shifts in the mood and emotional activation of the client (2012) (see the Resources section at the end of the book). Observing and then gently commenting on what is noticed opens an opportunity for the client to deepen their awareness of their somatic state, and conversely, the practitioner can attune to a cue to pull back.

> ...the feeling tone underpinning the client's experience in the moment is palpably present in his or her language of gesture, proxemics, verbal, co-verbal and nonverbal expression. Simply articulating this implicit emotion and inviting elaboration ("I notice your jaw is trembling when you say that. What's happening for you right now" or "If those tears could speak, what would they tell us?") is often enough to deepen the client's self-awareness, prompting symbolization of new meaning and pre-condition to its further negotiation. (Neimeyer 2012, p.6)

Moving is another way to release stuck energy. I often invite clients to stand, to swing their arms, to shake out their limbs to release what they have been holding back. I do this along with them so that they can feel comfortable. We also might stretch up and then reach down, using our breath to enhance the energy flow. Moving around is a good way to move emotions and can even lessen the effects of a panic attack.

There are several somatic activities in Part Two that can help the client move with their grief, and ground themselves when they are feeling out of control. These offer bereaved clients ways to release emotions using mindful techniques, including focus on being in the moment, noticing one's surroundings, tracking the fluctuations within the polyvagal nervous system, and a few simple movement exercises that nearly anyone can do. Feel free to modify the activity to fit the client's needs and abilities.

Mindfulness

The groundlessness IS the ground.

Moke Mokotoff, my husband

Mindfulness is, in its most basic form, simply becoming aware of the present moment. The act of tuning in, of paying attention to the state of the breath, the state of the body, and where you are, brings you to what is happening now. During times of extreme emotion, having simple skills to slow down, to calm down, is not only helpful; at times it is necessary. Mindfulness can also be grounding, which is important when a griever feels as if the ground has loosened under their feet. When we have lost our assumptive world and have not yet rebuilt new premises on which to operate, paying attention to this moment, right now, is a good strategy. After all, the present is really all we have. Encourage clients to spend some time just being with what is and where they are so that they can experience the calm that accompanies mindful attention, without grasping any particular thought or emotion.

Simple meditation techniques are also beneficial to grievers; however, attempting to sit quietly and apply strict ideas of what meditation might be can be problematic without guidance. Meditative techniques spring from spiritual and religious practices that often have rules about how you should sit, how you should think or not think, or even specific chants or hand movements (mudras) that accompany the practice. Meditative and contemplative practices can be found in Judaic, Christian, Islamic, Buddhist, and Hindu traditions. Be sensitive to the particular cultural and spiritual mindset of your client before introducing mindful practices, as some religious traditions are suspicious of different methods of contemplation.

I am actually not recommending any particular way to contemplate or even recommending meditation as a spiritual practice. I am not talking about any set spiritual way to approach the use of meditative techniques to reduce emotional and physical arousal. Rather, I am referring to mindful awareness, a simple noticing of breathing, posture, and thoughts that arise. Some of my clients have tried to sit in quiet meditation only to find themselves even more emotionally activated. This happened to me when I first tried to sit quietly, just a few months after my late husband died. We often apply rules we have heard about, and clients might think that they must sit for a certain amount of time or else they are not "doing it right." While this might be true in a classical spiritual sense, this is not what is recommended here.

Thanatologist and yoga therapist, Heather Stang, MA, offers a program using mindfulness and guided visualization for grief in her book, *Mindfulness & Grief* (2018). She guides the reader through eight themes that can be engaged with over an eight-week period. Using mindful awareness, conscious relaxation, self-compassion, and courage enables the griever to become more present with their experience and to relax into an open-hearted attitude towards their own grief. Getting unstuck, finding meaning, and looking towards transformation helps the bereaved person move through their emotions and begin to engage with their life, or at least to consider how they might be able to do so. The eighth session focuses on maintaining mindfulness and continuing to practice the techniques she offers. Practitioners can use all or parts of her program in counseling and can encourage clients who are interested in learning more about mindfulness and meditation to investigate it further for themselves (see the Resources section at the end of this book).

The polyvagal nervous system

Our nervous system reacts to stimuli even before we are rationally aware of this reaction. The polyvagal cluster of nerves connects our brain to all our organs, heart, lungs, diaphragm, intestines, and also our eyes, ears, and facial muscles. Vagal means wandering, and an anatomical diagram of this system shows the various nerves that make up the polyvagal system wandering all through our central body. It is through this collection of branches and fibers that impulses are sent which stimulate the fight, flight, or freeze response and also cause reactions in heart rate, blood pressure, and sensations of heat or cold. The polyvagal nerves are home to what some refer to as the secondary brain or the gut brain.

This primitive system evolved as humans evolved. Having an activating internal system enabled ancient humans to get out of the way of charging tigers or swooping eagles, or to stand their ground and fight when attacked. This survival system is still within modern humans even though it is unlikely that there is a charging wild animal chasing you down the street.

The polyvagal system developed in a triune way. The lowest part of the nerves is connected to the gastrointestinal system and is mostly unmyelinated. This part of the system is called the dorsal vagal and is related to the freeze response. When a person is in a dorsal state, they are immobilized, even collapsed. They may feel dull, numb, and unable to move or take any action. They may curl up and go to sleep. The dorsal state is a disconnected one, and in grief, there are times when going dorsal is protective and necessary. A person in this state may comment that they don't feel anything and have trouble getting out of bed to face the day.

The next part of the vagal system is the sympathetic vagal state. This is where the person feels mobilized to make a quick choice between fight or flight. They feel motivated and active, but also defensive and tense. Their eyes may open wide or narrow, but they are not connecting through eye contact; rather, they are in a self-protective mode. The nerves connected to the inner ear close off nearly all but the lowest and highest sound, as the body primes itself for danger.

In fact, safety is what this ancient nervous system is designed for. The dorsal and sympathetic nervous reactions keep us from harm, and alert us to danger signs so that we can defend against them or disappear by collapsing to the ground.

In grief, when the emotional, psychic, and cognitive functions are adversely affected, this freeze, flight, or fight system is stimulated and sometimes reacts to small stimuli, as if there is a threat. This is the classic, overblown reaction that is stimulated in cases of PTSD, and there are many grievers who react in a similar way, especially in early grief and particularly in cases of sudden death or traumatic death such as homicide, accident, or suicide. It is helpful to know that this is a normal physiological reaction to perceived threat. By recognizing it as such, it may be easier for the person affected to apply a "vagal brake," or to use a strategy to move them out of this uncomfortable state and sometimes inappropriate reaction.

The third part of the polyvagal system is where this vagal brake can be applied. The ventral vagal state is one of connection. The eyes open and connect with another person. The ears tune into vocal prosody, and the heart slows. The person feels calmer and no longer perceives the situation as dangerous. In the ventral state, a person is better equipped to make choices about how to respond to a triggering sound or memory.

Therapist Deb Dana has written a book, *Polyvagal Theory in Therapy* (2018), which clearly explains how this system works and how practitioners can use this information to help highly activated clients. She suggests bringing awareness to notice which state the person is in, to apply self-compassion for that state, and then to look for "triggers" to understand what caused the dorsal or sympathetic reaction. Self-compassion can lead to curiosity, which leads to inquiry, leading to discovery. By noticing what is activating us to react as if we are threatened, we can begin to learn how to break the pattern of fight, flight, or freeze and move ourselves into the ventral vagal state, where we can speak and listen as we share our stories.

> Deepening into curiosity and active inquiry brings us into possibility. Curiosity has been called the opening of our heart intuition. Here in the flow of a ventral vagal state, the options and outcomes are limitless. This is where regulating, resourcing, reciprocity, reconnection, repatterning, and re-storying can happen! (Dana 2018, p.43)

Dana recommends that we invite our clients to notice what lifts them out of their collapsed or aggressively activated states by focusing on "glimmers" (p.67). These could include noticing beauty in nature, feeling gratitude, recalling fond memories, or simply paying attention to breath. If triggers are cues of danger, glimmers are cues of safety. By focusing in on what is happening within our body, we can also tune in to what moves us into a calmer more connected and less activated state.

When I explain polyvagal arousal to my clients, they connect with the concept. We all go through aspects of freeze, flight, or fight, and hopefully we have also felt calm and connected with others at various points in our lives. By explaining this as a natural, protective reaction within our nervous system, clients can let go of judgment on themselves. They can also begin to notice what triggers them and how they can help themselves move out of a state they are uncomfortable with or to allow themselves to relax into that state for a while.

The somatic activities in Part Two of this book can be used to observe polyvagal responses. There is also an activity to track which state the client is in and how they might fluctuate between dorsal, sympathetic, and ventral states during their grieving process. I also recommend learning more about how the body holds emotion and trauma, and to discover your own ways to help clients notice and work through the tension.

MEANING MAKING

When someone significant dies and our assumptions shatter, life seems to lose its meaning. If the person who died is integral to our life, how we view ourselves and what we do in the world also seems to have died. The widow or widower not only loses their life partner, but all the plans, dreams, and hopes for the future are also lost. Perhaps the breadwinner of the family is now gone, along with the confidant, the sounding board, the person who brought balance to parenting, the one who cooked all the meals and knew everyone else's schedule. When a parent dies, the surviving child might lose their closest supporter, their cheerleader, their advisor, their daycare provider. When a child dies, potential dies along with the child, and the parent is bereft not only of their child but also of their hopes for accomplishment and success which that child was supposed to achieve. There will be no graduations or weddings, no grandchildren to carry on the family traditions. Or if there are grandchildren, there may no longer be that father to walk them down the aisle or the mother to guide them through their lives. We don't believe that our children should die before us, so the injustice and unfairness of this also affects our feeling that the world makes sense. A bereaved parent may find some comfort in the friends of their child, but this will also be a reminder of what they will not have, as those friends go to graduate school, get married, and have children and successful careers.

We build our lives in conjunction with others. We make plans, share secrets, vent in private to that special person. Now they are gone. With them went those hopes and dreams, and now the grievers often feel that life has little meaning. This is taken personally as a loss of purpose. Life seems to have broken into many pieces, leaving the person feeling as if they are sitting among the rubble of their expectations and hopes.

Finding meaning in the midst of tragedy and difficult life circumstances was discussed brilliantly in Viktor Frankl's *Man's Search for Meaning* (2006). Frankl's experience as a young person in a concentration camp is described therein, with an emphasis on finding beauty, a sense of connection and actual meaning within the violent existence in the camp. He believed that the motivator of a person's life force, the reason a person is able to continue to live in the midst of such horror is precisely that—a quest for meaning in life. Frankl felt that each person is pulled towards discovering meaning within life experiences, and that if this meaning can be viewed as positive in some way, the person will be able to live and even thrive in spite of adverse circumstances.

This view is also prevalent in thanatology. Dr Robert Neimeyer lost his own father when he was young. The impact of this event on his own life propels his work, and he has spent years investigating bereavement and healing, encouraging many of his students to explore and define how we grieve. Neimeyer's ideas and methods of working with the bereaved have had a major influence on grief counseling; his approach is sensitive and creative, and makes use of storytelling, dream work, and ways to move beyond acute grief and into the realm of living life. He believes that finding meaning again after loss is a critical part of the healing process.

Asking someone to find meaning immediately after someone dies can be problematic. Rather, finding meaning and purpose is better addressed after the person has moved through their own grief process for a while. Discovering meaning is an exploration of how death has affected life and is part of the inquiry into how the griever wishes to live now.

Bereavement is a process of adaptation. At first, the raw emotion overrides almost everything else. Slowly, the griever takes small steps towards re-engaging in their lives with friends, family, and work. They may find that activities they used to enjoy now feel hollow and devoid of importance. Their sense of purpose and meaning has been intrinsically tied to the person who is gone. If they were carers of the deceased, they may have given a lot of time, energy, and focus to this caregiving, and when the person dies, the griever has also lost a job that gave them meaning, which was keeping their loved one alive or at least comfortable.

Finding meaning again requires that the griever first makes sense of what has happened. By allowing them to question the events, to question what they and others did around the time of death, they can begin to make sense of how they have been affected. They may consider the adjustments they have had to make and how their life has changed. They can even reflect on the loss of meaning and purpose in order to explore possibilities for reconstructing their life.

> When you seek meaning for or an understanding of what you are experiencing, you actively reconstruct your world to accommodate the changes you have experienced and continue to go through. The empowerment that comes from realizing how active a role you play in the construction of your world is the vehicle for harnessing the transformative power of grief. (Kumar 2005, p.83)

Meaning making can be accomplished in different ways. For some, meaning is found in knowing the relationship mattered to the deceased. Meaning can be found in observing how the deceased impacted the world during their life or how the griever was supported, changed, or cared for. Meaning may be found in activities that relate to the person who died, such as donating something to others who might need it or enjoy its use.

Clients can be guided to discover meaning by noticing how they have developed a sense of purpose in other circumstances in their lives. The ability to move through grief and to recognize growth both from the relationship (or in some cases, in spite of it) and from your own life experience is, in and of itself, a purposeful activity.

As a reconstructivist psychologist, Neimeyer's view of rebuilding life after loss includes retelling your story in a restorative way in order to discover deeper meaning within the relationship to the deceased. Restorative retelling allows grievers to reconstruct narratives that are beneficial to themselves. Neimeyer uses dreams, metaphor, poetry, and other expressive modalities to develop meaning and a sense of purpose. Find more about working with narratives in the activities in Part Two.

Chapter 5

THE *WHOLE* PROCESS—USING DIFFERENT LENSES

When the client feels shattered by grief, they may long to get back to life as they knew it before. Rediscovering a sense of wholeness is part of the rebuilding process. The disruption of life as they knew it, the hole that might feel present now without that significant person, creates a longing for what life was like before and now is no longer possible. What is possible is to rebuild your own life over time, to pick up the pieces and examine them. Figuring out how to live again is part of the challenge of grief. Looking at grief through different lenses offers several ways to work towards restoring a sense of balance and more stable footing. Please remember that this process will take time, and that if some of these suggestions receive a strong negative reaction, it could be that the client is simply not ready to consider them yet. Grief is not going to be resolved in five easy steps in six months. Using the word WHOLE as an acronym, the lenses peer into the following concepts: What Happened and Who Am I? Help! How do I do this?; Opening to Emotion; Learning to Live Fully Again; and Exploring the Past to Experience the Future.

NARRATIVE LENS: WHAT HAPPENED? WHO AM I?

We know each other by the stories we tell, and when we have difficulty, telling the story of what happened and how we have been affected is compelling. There is an adage that says we must tell the story 72 times in order to heal. I don't know if this number is correct, but I do find clients need to tell their story. They need to be heard, they need to talk it through in order to believe it really happened.

Working with narratives is also a compelling way to help clients understand what has changed in their lives, how they feel about it, and what they might be able to do. How they tell the story, the nuances they include, as well as crafting a different narrative could also shift how they feel about what happened. There are many ways to tell the story of loss. It can be told from a factual point of view but after a while, the client might become stuck in this story. There is also the story of the relationship itself and of the gifts received and the gifts given (by gifts, I mean what has been gained and learned in that relationship).

In addition to the story of how the person died, the client can be encouraged to share stories of the life they shared. Ask how they met or to describe a vacation or a favorite place. What was the most important thing they learned from this person, and how will they bring this knowledge forward? Ask for a funny story or a reflection on how that person lived their life. By using narrative, the client will be able to express how they feel, what they did, and how they have grown from being in this relationship. They can also be encouraged to bring photographs into the counseling office to share, which will also lead to more storytelling.

A client will also benefit from viewing their story in a more magical way. Being playful is very helpful when a person is feeling sad and heavy. Humor, laughter, and funny stories all have a place in grief healing. Imagining themselves as a superhero and telling the story from that perspective can help a bereaved person feel empowered. Telling a fairy tale story can have an impact on how the client feels about the life of the deceased, or might enable the client to see their struggle with grief in heroic terms.

Stream of consciousness writing is another way to work with narrative. Filling in a circle with one run-on sentence is one way to get into the flow of narrative.

In addition to the story we tell about our lives, we often define ourselves by who we are connected to and by what we do. When someone dies, the roles we play in the world shift. Along with the sense that the world is unstable, many grievers often question their identity. Who am I if I am no longer a wife? Am I still a parent now that my child has died? Who am I now that I am experiencing all these crazy emotions?

Helping clients identify aspects of self, define roles, and notice qualities that they already have offers them a way to see how they view themselves. There may be qualities that are diametrically opposed but the practitioner can notice connections, strengths, and skills. For example, if the person states that they are angry and that they procrastinate, you might ask how their anger might stimulate them to get over their tendency to put things off.

A journal is a wonderful container for narratives. Within its pages, a person can craft variations on old stories, shifting the view from what happened to its impact. By making choices in how the story unfolds, the writer has the opportunity to develop new narratives. I often give a journal prompt at the end of a session for my client to ponder and explore, either in conversation or in a journal. Then we can discuss their response in our next session.

A journal is also a useful tool for discovering meaning. Is there something the client always wanted to learn, some place they would like to go? Would engaging in a new activity provide a sense of purpose in their life? Even if they are not yet ready to try these things, the journal can hold lists of possibilities, even photographs of countries to travel to, pictures of potential things to do.

The griever may also reflect on how their priorities have now changed now. Within the pages of the journal, gratitude can be expressed, or life lessons explored. The possibilities of gifts within this loss may be considered and written about in the journal. All these journaling activities can help the bereaved person explore their inner responses to this loss and can lead them to make choices on how they want their life to be (Lichtenthal and Neimeyer 2012).

ACTIVE LENS: HELP! HOW DO I DO THIS?

There is no one correct way to live this. Others have come before you, and others will come after, but no one carried grief—or love—in the same way you do. Grief is as individual as love. There's nothing to do but experiment.
It's all a work in progress.

Megan Devine

While I heartily endorse expressing emotions, grievers also need something to do. The dual process demonstrates this important fact—that not only is it common for people to oscillate between feeling and doing; it is also necessary. You cannot weep and wail for hours and hours without becoming completely exhausted.

Unfortunately, grief often affects a person cognitively. It is common to have difficulty concentrating, to start a task, and then forget how to complete it. People put their keys in the refrigerator or the juice in the cabinet. It is helpful for our clients to know that this is normal; the amount of energy it takes to grieve takes its toll on the brain and the body.

Because of the effects on cognition and concentration, accomplishing normal tasks seems difficult for grievers, especially in the first year of grief. Strategies for getting things done in a timely fashion are important since there are some things that cannot be set aside for too long, such as adequate nutrition, sleep, taking care of yourself as well as the house, children, pets, etc. And in most cases, the griever must return to work fairly soon after a death and is often expected to perform as if nothing happened.

The fact that ordinary activities are so hard to undertake can make a person feel incompetent and insecure. Clients can be guided towards coming up with strategies that help them manage daily tasks such as making lists, reducing how much they take on at one time, and practicing a gentler attitude towards themselves. If the task list is very long and seems overwhelming, encourage them to prioritize the list and to check off one or two things a day. I also recommend that my clients congratulate themselves on accomplishing even one thing and not focusing on the 20 other things left to do on the list. One by one, over time, the list will be whittled down. This is also a mirror of a valid approach to the early part of grieving—taking it one hour at a time, one day at a time, makes it more manageable.

Clients can identify the people who are supportive by engaging in some of the creative exercises in Part Two. Once they know whom they can rely on, they may be able to solicit help from their social support in the form of some meal preparation or assistance with picking up the children from activities.

It is often hard for normally competent people to ask for help, yet grief is a time when it is appropriate. Condolences often come with an offer to help, in the form of a "call me if you need me" statement. This is problematic for a grieving person who is unlikely to pick up the phone when they need something. Instead, if they had a short list of things that could be delegated, they might be able to respond in the moment the offer is made. A friend who goes to the corner store every morning could be invited to pick up the griever's newspaper or a gallon of milk once in a while.

FEELING LENS: OPENING TO EMOTION

Almost everything I've learned and achieved has come from being a student of discomfort. Go against the grain and feel your feelings. It will mature you. The way is through.

Victoria Zaitz

Emotions are the most obvious reactions to grief. Witnessing someone else in an extreme emotional state is hard on practitioners because the impulse is to soothe them and to try to help them fix their "problem." But there is no fix for grief, and if we expect clients to be stoic or not to express their deep feelings, we are doing them a disservice.

Not everyone feels wracked with sorrow after someone dies. They may have had a problematic relationship, or perhaps they were not really that close. A lack of emotional reaction can cause the client some distress since society is filled with expectations that try to dictate how we should feel and how we should appropriately express these feelings. There are examples in films, in literature, and even in advertising that suggest what "normal grief" looks like. More often than not, the external message is that we should suppress certain feelings as if emotion is socially unacceptable. This message comes in the guise of "thinking positively" as in "You should just put a smile on your face and then you will feel better" or "It's not that bad, now, is it?" "You are young, you can find another" or "She lived a long life, you have nothing to cry about" dismiss how the griever actually feels, making them question their own internal response to the loss.

And then there are "bad" emotions that are strong but that are considered negative. Yet these feelings have a lot of power, rooted as they are in the type of connection and the position the deceased had in a person's life. If a grieving person tries to pretend that anger, fear, panic, or worry don't exist, these feelings may fester and boil just beneath the surface. It is a better strategy to give them voice, express them fully, and then they can be released, until they rise up again.

One client came to see me six months after the death of her father. She had been telling herself that she could handle her grief even though she spent many hours crying day and night. Her attempts to suppress her sorrow when she was at work were turning it into rage, and she found herself having arguments with her co-workers and filled with resentment at everyone who did not share her grief or who was insensitive to how she was feeling, even though she was not talking to anyone about it. Her father had been ill for many years and comments made by her co-workers and friends cued her to the expectation that she should not be feeling his death so flagrantly.

I invited her to tell me about her father and their relationship. I sympathized and validated all her emotional expressions, which were loud and weepy. She flipped between sharing how wonderful he was to her and her son to wailing about how much she missed him. She went through boxes of tissues as she finally let out what she was pushing down. I used calming techniques towards the end of the session so that she could feel grounded as well as relieved of some of what she was holding. She began journaling every day, writing to her father to tell him about her life. Slowly, over many sessions, she became less labile, more engaged in her work life, and began to feel like she had more control in her life.

Allowing your office to be a safe place to hold emotional expression enables your grieving client to feel comfortable. This will also help them feel supported when they cry, wail, or express their loss with yearning, tears, anxiety, or anger. Giving them room and time to release these emotions will enable them to move through them. Gently encouraging regulation of these emotions after they have been released for a while will enable them to witness their own ability to calm themselves. Noting how they are able to take care of themselves during and after an emotional release shows them how resilient they actually are. Guiding them in a fluctuation between release and regulation allows them to discover a balance between being involved with what they lost and developing how they want to live their life now.

Use some of the somatic interventions in the activities in Part Two to help a person release their emotions. Try some prompting questions or ask them to share a memory or something they are grateful for. What good will come out of this grief? What have they learned from being in relationship with the deceased? What are the gifts they received from that person or what did they learn that they can apply now?

Exploring the various emotions and noticing what triggers them is another way to help grieving clients. Grieving is often an experience of flipping from one emotion to another at a rapid pace, and pausing to notice if any of these feelings could be enhanced to help cope with another feeling is good practice. Remind the client to breathe. Remind them to move, gently, with that breath. And be sure to have tissues to hand.

RESTORATIVE LENS: LEARNING TO LIVE FULLY AGAIN

When you come to the edge of your comfort zone, push against it. Your comfort zone will expand.

Eben Coenen, my son

When someone dies, particularly if is a spouse or partner or a child, it is very hard for the grieving person to imagine their lives without them. So much has changed; the roles have shifted. The person that shared confidences and responsibilities, provided back-up, and needed guidance, is gone. If it was a parent, they have lost a source of family history.

Learning to live life fully after someone integral to your life dies is daunting for many people. At the same time, it is an opportunity for personal inquiry. What was important about the way life was lived before this person died? What has changed since they died? Which of these changes continue to be uncomfortable or difficult? Which of these changes are actually positive, or can, at least, be handled without too much stress?

When a person sets out to rebuild their life, there are many factors to consider. These are the building blocks, so to speak—while the house has crumbled, the foundation is probably still strong. The scattered pieces of life as it was can be used to rebuild once they are identified as aspects that are still useful. As the griever tries new things, applies personal resilience, slowly, the reconstruction of their life begins to take shape.

As counselors, therapists, and researchers delve deeper into the realm of bereavement and how to assist clients, the subject of complicated grief arises. Colin Murray Parkes and Holly Prigerson developed one of the first scales to measure whether grief is complicated or not (2010). Dr Katherine Shear at Columbia University in New York has developed a model for treating complicated grief that occurs in 7–9 percent of bereaved people, according to her research (see the Resources section at the end of the book). Complicated grief usually includes enmeshed relationships, difficult attachments and often, other psychological issues that underlie and pre-date the event that caused this grief. Cases of multiple losses also generate more complicated reactions.

In my practice, when older psychological issues arise during the grief process, I might refer my client to a clinician who is more adept at treating those issues. Often, I work in conjunction with a therapist while I focus on the grief itself.

Generally speaking, 9 percent is a relatively small incidence of actual complicated grief, which is diagnosable and requires specific treatment. The DSM-V, the diagnostic tool put out by American Psychiatric Association, uses the term "persistent grief disorder" and suggests that treatment would be required if symptoms do not subside within six months.

As a thanatologist, the idea that grief should be resolved within six months is anathema. While there are people who are not deeply affected by their loss due to the age of the person who died or due to circumstances in their relationship, the majority of people who seek counseling for their grief will feel grief symptoms for at least a year, and most likely for several years. Life as they knew it has been irrevocably changed, so in reality, the loss of a spouse, sibling, parent, or close friend will impact them for the rest of their lives. Every anniversary of the death, every birthday or new milestone that the deceased is missing will bring up some grief, whether it is a full-blown reaction or a small pinprick of nostalgia. They are missed now that they are gone and they will be missed forever.

Counseling the bereaved helps them move through the pain of loss, and the rawness and overpowering sensations that are experienced in the beginning will slowly subside. While some of these early reactions may appear complicated, helping clients parse out their own complicated feelings eventually leads them towards a resolution of the emotion while not necessarily a resolution of grief itself. When a parent has died and the grandchild marries, there are natural feelings of loss and longing that arise, even if they died a long time ago. A widow might choose to live alone but might feel reawakened grief when friends celebrate wedding anniversaries or when she sees older couples holding hands. Widowed people who repartner might experience confusion and some complicated feelings of guilt, even though they are committed to the new relationship.

These circumstances may feel complex, but they are not necessarily complicated grief. Complicated grief is more of an inability to effectively move through the grieving process over a long period of time. Please be sensitive to your client and pay attention to areas where the client seems stuck. Use creative strategies to help them explore different ways of viewing their grief, and their past, which opens up new ways of envisioning their future.

TRANSFORMATIVE LENS: EXPLORING THE PAST TO EXPERIENCE THE FUTURE

The idea that we can be transformed by adversity is both a welcome one and a problematic concept. In reality, loss cannot be transformed because the person who died is not going to come back. Our lives change and we can choose to grow, perhaps even be forced to shift what we do and how we feel by the circumstances created by the loss. While I am generally on the side of growth, I am also deeply aware that the death of someone close to you will always feel dissonant and in many cases, unfair. Psychotherapist and widow, Megan Devine, talks about the culture of positivity in her book, *It's OK that You're NOT OK* (2017):

> There's a gag order on telling the truth, in real life and in our fictional accounts. As a culture, we don't want to hear that there are things that can't be fixed. As a culture, we don't want to hear that there is some pain that never gets redeemed. Some things we learn to live with, and that's not the same as everything working out in the end. No matter how many rainbows and butterflies you stick into the narrative, some stories just don't work out. (Devine 2017, p.34)

Devine is making an important point. The pressure to think positively is often untenable for the bereaved. Yet, when a grieving person begins to choose life in the midst of their sadness over the death of someone, they do begin to transform how they feel. As they begin to relocate their connection to the deceased, placing them more in memory than in the present, what they do and how they live also shifts. This is what I mean by the transformative lens—it is a lens through which a grieving person views their life in connection to their past and opens them to viewing their future. The transformative lens allows them to see that they *have* a future, in spite of the loss. (See the Resources section at the end of the book for information on Megan Devine.)

How we cope with grief, death, and life changes have some roots in how our family and our culture approaches these situations. Once the griever has moved through the early, emotionally charged part of grief, when they are ready to think about their own future, exploring their family's patterns of behavior during difficult times can offer some insights. It could be these are inspiring or the opposite, but noticing how our forebears coped with life's changes might be interesting, noticing how they handled adverse circumstances such as poverty, pogroms, wars, or relocation offers understanding that can be applied to grief.

My own grandparents were forced out of Nazi Germany and lost their livelihood, their homes, and a good deal of their possessions. One of the first things my Opa did when he emigrated to the USA was to purchase dozens of books on American history so that he could learn about his new country. This attitude has influenced how I approach any difficulty in my life; I seek to learn as much as I can by learning how others handled similar situations.

Exploring the relationship with the deceased can also inform how to re-engage in life. There may be some personal quality of theirs that the griever might want to enhance in their own life. Perhaps there was a cause they associated with or the circumstances of their death may stimulate the bereaved person to raise money for. Many people establish mini-marathons in honor of their deceased person; some even start foundations. Mothers Against Drunk Driving (MADD) is an example of this; the MISS Foundation was started by psychologist Joanne Cacciatore after the stillbirth of her child, and provides support, education, and advocacy for bereaved parents; the Yellow Dress Foundation, created by Sharon Strause and her husband Don, holds a golf tournament every year, raising money to prevent suicide.

Honoring the deceased person can be done privately in the form of an area in the home containing photographs, special items of meaning, and perhaps a candle to light. This kind of altar is commonly arranged in some cultures as a way of remembering, having a place to speak to the dead, and also to create a felt sense of connection, an actual place to say something to them even though they are gone. Others find it important to visit the cemetery for the same reason, bringing flowers or even a lawn chair to sit with them, perhaps reading a letter or a portion of their journal.

What did the deceased enjoy in their lives? One client of mine, whose mother was an avid piano player, donated her mother's piano to a local community center in need of one. Another donated her daughter's furniture to an afterschool program focused on empowering girls. Others plant gardens with favorite flowers or plant a tree to remember them by. The garden or a special tree can also have a bench where the griever can sit to commune with nature and with their memories. While some may view this as focusing on the past, in fact, remembering well and with gratitude can help a griever develop positive perspectives, opening them to possible ways to move forward after loss.

Exploring the past, its connections and history, enables the griever to locate the deceased within the context of this history. Learning family stories and sharing them also contributes to this contextual scenario, permitting the griever to release some longing as their loved one is remembered and celebrated. This, in turn, contributes to a release of the past to some extent, which then clears the way for looking towards the future.

How does the griever imagine their life now? What would they like to do with it? If it is hard to envision, there is an opportunity to color in that blank slate. They might begin in a small way, perhaps by thinking about activities they used to enjoy, and deciding to try one or two of them again. There may be something they have always been interested in; how might they learn about that and where? Perhaps they always dreamed of going up in a hot air balloon, or vacationing somewhere. Simply rearranging furniture or painting a room a new color can help the griever feel differently about their environment, which will help them feel better about enlisting in their work, re-energizing friendships, and even shifting how they approach their daily lives.

The idea of transforming your life after a loss is similar to the concept of post-traumatic growth (PTG). PTG is a method of working with trauma and difficult life situations, developed and researched by Richard G. Tedeschi and Lawrence G. Calhoun. While they clarified ways to help clients find ways to grow from their experiences, they point out that this idea is as old as humanity has existed:

> ...for thousands of years there have been stories of positive changes in individuals and societies in general as a result of suffering and distress. The potential for transformative positive change from the experience of great challenge and despair is referred to in texts and teachings of all major religions and is reflected in writings of ancient philosophers and scholars of other disciplines. Drawing on this wisdom, old and new, and combined with contemporary knowledge gained through empirical evidence of various types, it is clear that a majority of people who experience trauma recover, are resilient to the impact of potential trauma, or experience growth. (Tedeschi *et al.* 2018, p.7)

The possibility of growth can be found within grief as well. While it was an unwanted circumstance, as the survivor of loss begins to re-engage in their life, they may notice what is different and how they have changed. They may consciously make choices about how to facilitate change, whether it is subtle as in not being bothered by petty annoyances anymore because death has taught them not to waste time, or whether it is a choice of where to live or whether to change occupations or go back to school to do something different.

Another transformative possibility is to consider personality traits. What aspects of personality are useful and what no longer works? How can the useful ways of being in the world be enhanced, and how can the habits that no longer serve be reduced?

And what about the person who died—are there aspects of them that the griever has incorporated into themselves? Identifying the threads of connection, the things learned in relationship to the person who died, the griever can bring aspects of their character forward into their own lives.

Chapter 6

COMPASSION IN ACTION—*KARUNA*

I call my grief counseling practice The Karuna Project because my late husband wrote this word on the top of his letters. *Karuna* is a Sanskrit word which means active compassion, a necessary component of counseling the bereaved. As practitioners working with clients coping with death and other deep losses, applying active compassion fosters a nonjudgmental attitude towards the client. This generates a safe haven in which the client can express their loss, their reactions to it, and even voice thoughts that they might label as "crazy." It is normal for grievers to repeat such statements as, "I can't believe she is dead" or "My life is over" or "My life has no meaning anymore." When they spend hours crying uncontrollably or when they say they feel numb and have not cried at all, our job is to listen patiently. Normalizing grief by accepting its expressions in whatever form they take encourages deeper inquiry into the grief experience itself. The client is reminded that they are not losing their mind because they are distressed by the death; in fact, the depth of their grief is directly related to the depth of their feeling for the deceased.

Self-care is a compassionate practice too. Paying attention to the breath to calm down or using simple grounding techniques makes it easier to cope with grief later. Just as we might oscillate between feeling and doing, a person in grief can move between allowing their emotions to flow and engaging in actions that generate some peace and relaxation.

Human beings are hardwired to look for threats and in a way, we tend to lean towards the negative. Focusing on something that is pleasurable and allowing the pleasure, beauty, or sensations associated with it to permeate our whole being actually makes new connections in our brains. Bringing fresh flowers into the home or infusing a pleasant smelling essential oil can enliven the senses and lighten the mood. Encourage clients to be compassionate towards themselves, without expending too much effort. If they have a favorite food or beverage, they could enjoy it, taking a bit more time than they normally would to savor the taste and take it in as a gift.

Practitioners can demonstrate the principles of *karuna* through compassionate presence. What a bereaved person needs more than anything is someone who will be with them, who will not judge or tell them how to fix their unfixable grief. By hearing them through even the craziest thoughts, allowing them to voice these thoughts in order to parse them out and move beyond them, the bereaved person can begin to blaze a trail through the unknown journey of their own grief process. Then we can be an "expert companion" offering not only active listening but also some strategies and creative explorations to try.

PART TWO

We really can learn to integrate loss and change, infuse ourselves with wisdom, apply self-love, liberally and skillfully, investigate and allow our mysteries and experience the pains as well as the gladnesses of life.

SARK (Susan Ariel Rainbow Kennedy)

All pages marked with ✗ can be photocopied and downloaded from https://library.jkp.com/ redeem using the voucher code GYOTEKE

Chapter 7

CREATIVE ACTIVITIES

These creative activity sheets can be used within a counseling session and then discussed with the client. They can also be given as "homework" for the client to do in between sessions. I offer them to my clients and allow five or ten minutes for them to complete the activity, and then we talk about it. Or, they might discuss their response while they are engaging with the diagram. Some people simply hold the activity sheet and look at it, and then talk about their response to it without actually writing on the sheet.

I intend for these activities to be flexible and invite clients to ignore parts of them if they don't feel right at the moment. Some of the activities are more flexible than others and can be used at different times during the progression of the grief process. For example, the "Who Am I?" activity is useful in the beginning of counseling because it allows clients to begin to reflect on their own skills and resiliencies. It also allows practitioners to get to know what clients think about themselves. Later, this same wheel might be used to help clients explore how they feel about themselves after they have spent some time processing their grief and are beginning to re-engage in life. Comparing the two wheels will provide insight into that progress.

The somatic activities are meant to be approached gently and within the physical capacity of the client. I find it very helpful to mirror the client when I notice them holding tension, slumping in, or wrapping their arms around their bodies in a protective way. When I offer a somatic activity, I do it with them. We move chairs aside and step into an open space. I stand facing my client, breathing in unison with them, and moving with them. This helps to eliminate any self-consciousness about moving, and also makes the exercise a shared experience for us, which contributes to safety.

These activities are not offered in any particular order. I suggest that you, the practitioner, do these exercises yourself before you offer them to your grieving clients, so that you know how they feel and find your own way to present them. Each activity has an "instruction" page to guide you. These are my suggestions and are examples of how I use these activities and how I present them. Feel free to find your own way into these creative possibilities.

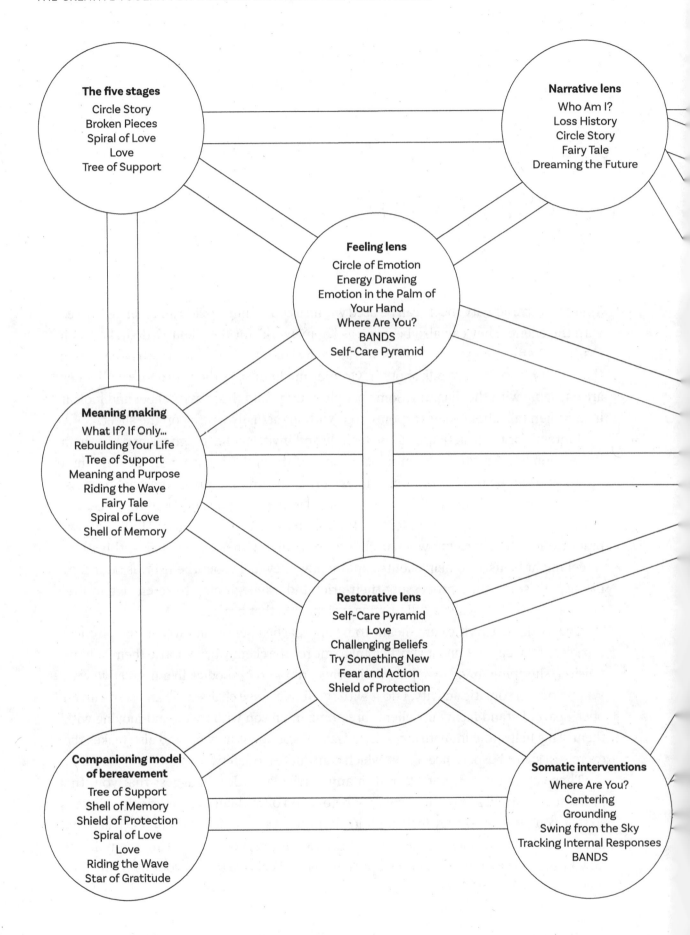

The five stages
Circle Story
Broken Pieces
Spiral of Love
Love
Tree of Support

Narrative lens
Who Am I?
Loss History
Circle Story
Fairy Tale
Dreaming the Future

Feeling lens
Circle of Emotion
Energy Drawing
Emotion in the Palm of
Your Hand
Where Are You?
BANDS
Self-Care Pyramid

Meaning making
What If? If Only...
Rebuilding Your Life
Tree of Support
Meaning and Purpose
Riding the Wave
Fairy Tale
Spiral of Love
Shell of Memory

Restorative lens
Self-Care Pyramid
Love
Challenging Beliefs
Try Something New
Fear and Action
Shield of Protection

**Companioning model
of bereavement**
Tree of Support
Shell of Memory
Shield of Protection
Spiral of Love
Love
Riding the Wave
Star of Gratitude

Somatic interventions
Where Are You?
Centering
Grounding
Swing from the Sky
Tracking Internal Responses
BANDS

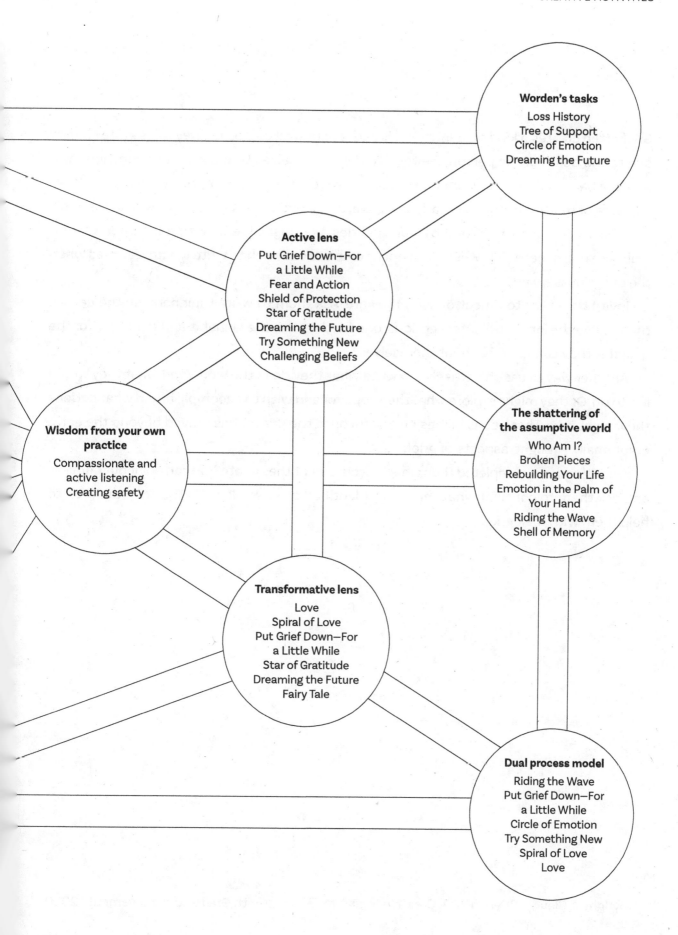

Worden's tasks

Loss History
Tree of Support
Circle of Emotion
Dreaming the Future

Active lens

Put Grief Down—For
a Little While
Fear and Action
Shield of Protection
Star of Gratitude
Dreaming the Future
Try Something New
Challenging Beliefs

**The shattering of
the assumptive world**

Who Am I?
Broken Pieces
Rebuilding Your Life
Emotion in the Palm of
Your Hand
Riding the Wave
Shell of Memory

**Wisdom from your own
practice**

Compassionate and
active listening
Creating safety

Transformative lens

Love
Spiral of Love
Put Grief Down—For
a Little While
Star of Gratitude
Dreaming the Future
Fairy Tale

Dual process model

Riding the Wave
Put Grief Down—For
a Little While
Circle of Emotion
Try Something New
Spiral of Love
Love

WHO AM I?

Grief often creates a kind of identity crisis in the bereaved person as their roles in life change due to the death of the person. We tend to define ourselves through our relationships, as a wife, husband or partner to someone, or as a parent or child. Now that the person who "made" us a wife or mother, husband or father, is gone, the question of "Who am I now?" looms large.

Who we are is also defined by our qualities. We might identify as a kind person or a stubborn one or both. This wheel is an open template on which to write whatever arises when the question is asked.

Invite the client to reflect on who they are. Ask them to write their name in the center, then to use the inner and outer sections, one for the roles they inhabit and the other for the qualities they can identify about themselves.

Another way to use this wheel is to write what they do in the world and what they would like to do. Or they might explore what they hope for and wish to accomplish, and what actions they might take. These possibilities are useful once the griever has moved beyond the early, emotionally wrought, aspects of grief.

Once they have completed their wheel, discuss what they wrote. You can point out parallels and ask them to consider what they have identified as possible skills they can tap into, to help them with their grief.

WHO AM I?

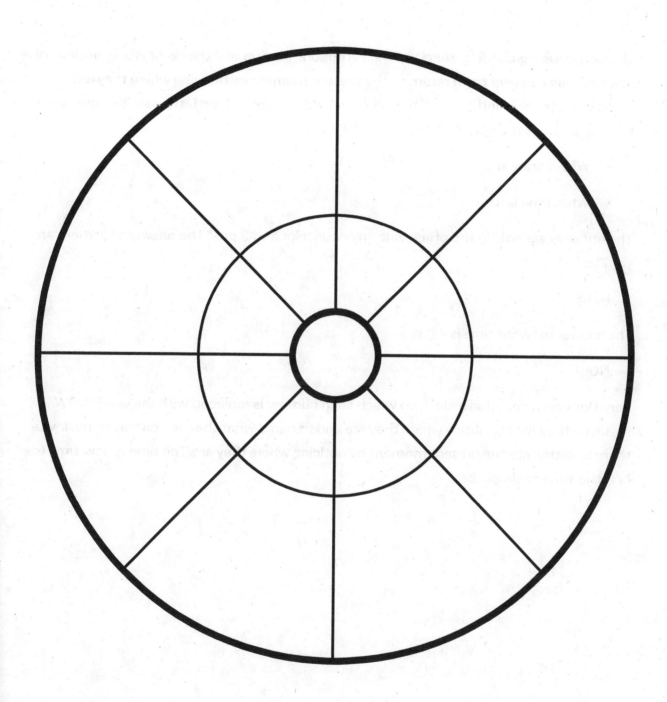

WHERE ARE YOU?

This activity is a grounding exercise. When emotions flare up or if the client is very anxious or agitated, you can help them return to the present moment by noticing where they are.

Spiritual teacher and writer of the book, *Be Here Now* (1971), Ram Dass, asks two questions to bring awareness to the present:

- Where are you?

- What time is it?

The answers are not "In the office with my counselor and 3 pm." The answer to "Where are you?" is

HERE.

The answer to "What time is it?" is

NOW.

Ram Dass even designed a clock on which each number is replaced with the word "NOW."

Invite the client to notice where they are and to name what they see on this sheet. Invite them to settle into the present moment by noticing where they are. The time is now, time to breathe, time to simply be.

WHERE ARE YOU?

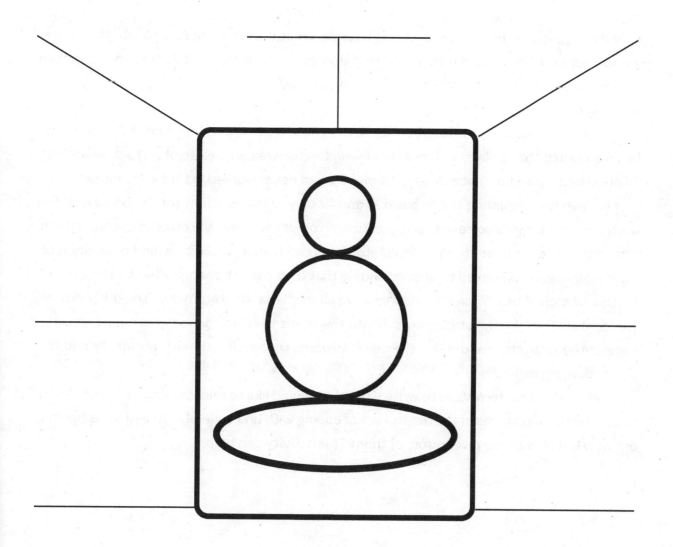

Be with what is

WHAT IF? IF ONLY... ▬▬▬▬▬▬▬▬▬

In early grief, it is common for questions to arise. What if the doctor had caught the cancer earlier? What if we had gone to a different doctor, tried an alternative treatment, gotten another opinion? What if it had not been raining that night? What if we had just stayed home that day?

"If only" questions also arise. The fact is, the grieving person wishes that the person who has died would still be alive, and their mind searches for a reason or a solution to this problem: "If only I had called her that evening;" "If only he had never worked in that warehouse."

I believe that exploring the "what if's" and "if only's" is important for the bereaved. It is better for them to give voice to these questions in order to release the emotions around them. After they have explored them, these statements can be subjected to a kind of reality test, slowly guiding the bereaved to understanding that they cannot change what has happened.

One branch of this "Y" can be used to write all the "what if" statements. The other branch can contain the "if only" statements. Invite the client to fill in these upper branches first. Look at them together and guide the client towards processing these statements and the accompanying regret.

Then, use the bottom stem to write what they would like to release, what they now know about the circumstances of the death. Part of coping with unanswerable questions is figuring out how to live with the discomfort of them. This activity can help.

WHAT IF? IF ONLY...

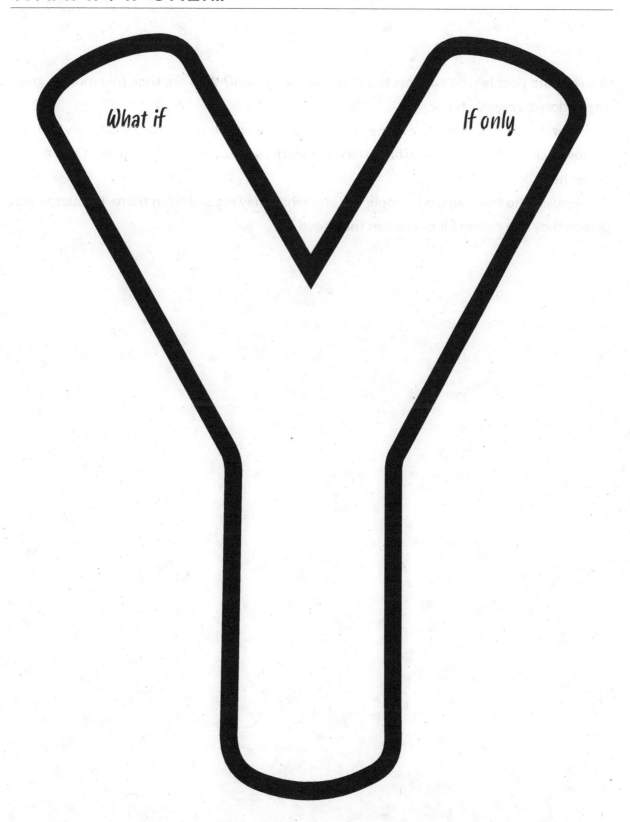

What if

If only

TREE OF SUPPORT ████████████████

Who are the people who support the client as they grieve? Who are their role models, their inspiration during this time?

Invite the client to write the names of these people on the tree. If they wish, they can use the lower circles for people who have been influential and supportive in their lives and are no longer here.

Discuss who their support people are and what they receive from them. Discuss which person they can call on for help when they need it.

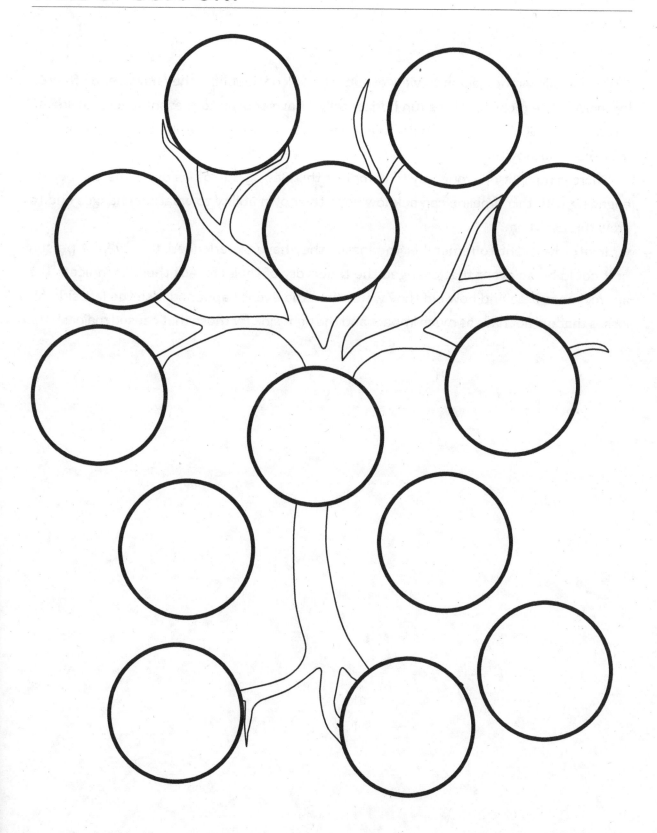

LOSS HISTORY

A timeline allows the person to view events and to consider how they have been affected by them. While most timelines run horizontally, I have chosen to present a vertical line. To me, a horizontal line seems to imply that life is linear while a vertical line could demonstrate resilience and growth.

There is no right or wrong way to complete this. Seeing the losses over time, the person engaging with this timeline can acknowledge their own ability to weather changes and to grow through them.

Invite the client to remember the losses they have experienced. It may be a person or it could be an event that changed the trajectory of their life. Ask them to indicate the approximate date and how old they were when the event happened. Use the left side for losses that did not have as much impact and the right side for those that caused major shifts.

LOSS HISTORY

EMOTION IN THE PALM OF YOUR HAND ▬▬▬

This activity creates distance from a strong emotion such as anger, anxiety, or fear. Its purpose is for the client to get in touch with this feeling, to allow it to arise with intensity, and to pay attention to how it is affecting them. Then they can begin to make choices about how involved with the feeling they want to be at this moment.

Ask the client to identify an emotion that is uncomfortable and maybe even overwhelming. Invite them to bring up the feeling, sense it within themselves, and then imagine they are placing it in the palm of their hand.

Imagine what the emotion feels like, sitting in the palm of the hand. Does it have a temperature? What color is it?

Invite the client to observe their emotion and identify aspects they associate with this strong feeling.

The emotion has a message. It may be connected to an event that happened long ago or something more recent. What does it remind them of? What is it trying to say? Allow the client to process these questions. Invite them to use the colors they have chosen as they draw/write on this sheet to express what arises from the inquiry.

When they feel complete, engage them in an exploration of how it felt to place their emotion in their hand. What did it have to tell them? What response do they have?

EMOTION IN THE PALM OF YOUR HAND

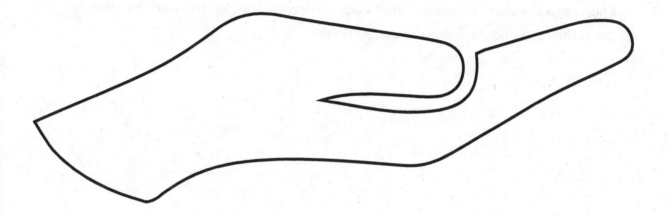

✘

BROKEN PIECES ▐▬▬▬▬▬▬▬▬▬▬▬▬▬▬▬▬

Grief can shatter the assumptions we build our lives on. When this happens, the world might seem broken.

Use this sheet for your client to explore what feels broken. Ask them to write what parts of them feel shattered or what has changed because of the death of their significant person.

They might also identify how they assumed their life would unfold, putting things like "growing old together" or "the vacation we planned for next summer" into the shards.

Encourage the client to use different colors when completing this activity. They can use words or they can doodle or draw in the sections.

BROKEN PIECES

What aspects of your life feel broken? Write them down inside the broken pieces.

REBUILDING YOUR LIFE ▮▮▮▮▮▮▮▮▮▮▮▮

If grief shatters the survivor, reconstructing their life out of the broken pieces might seem imperative. The shattered parts provide building blocks to use. These are the core values, the relationships that still exist, who the griever has become because of the person who died, and how they have coped with the loss.

This puzzle image is missing a piece. Reconstructing life after loss will still feel as if it is missing something. There is no getting around it; it is more something to learn to live with. The person who has died can be honored, can be remembered; the griever might even feel relief that they are gone if the relationship was charged and difficult. Yet:

- What are the important values you build your life on?

- What are your important qualities that make you who you are?

Write some of these ideas down inside the puzzle pieces.

CIRCLE OF EMOTION

This page is for expressing emotion, using color and shape. What it looks like is not as important as what it feels like. In fact, this can be done with eyes closed.

Invite the client to tune in to how they are feeling right now. Invite them to choose color, and to draw the emotions within the circle.

When they are finished they can reflect on the picture and share their reflection with you.

CIRCLE OF EMOTION

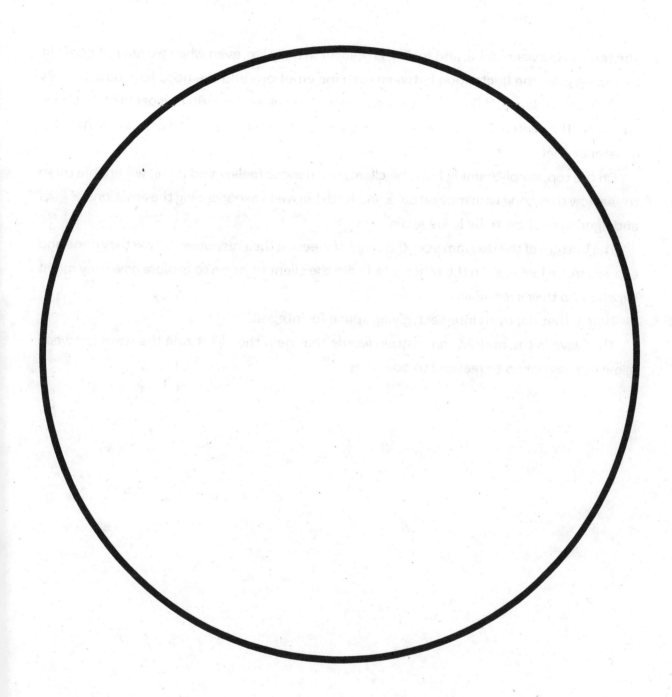

RIDING THE WAVE

The tension between doing and feeling is present in daily life, even when we are not grieving.

During grief, the fluctuation between extreme emotions and the need to attend to daily life feels very arduous. This activity provides space to explore the various aspects of that back and forth. The center lines can be used to express a more flowing way to cope with the roller coaster of grief.

On the top, simply naming how the client experiences feeling and doing will enable them to see how they cope with moving back and forth between experiencing the emotions of grief and figuring out how to be in life again.

The bottom of the diagram asks the client to deepen their response to how they cope and express these feelings. On the other side, invite the client to begin to explore how they might expand into their lives again.

Notice that the ovals intersect, giving space for integration.

The wave in the middle can contain words that help the client ride the wave between allowing themselves to feel and to do.

RIDING THE WAVE

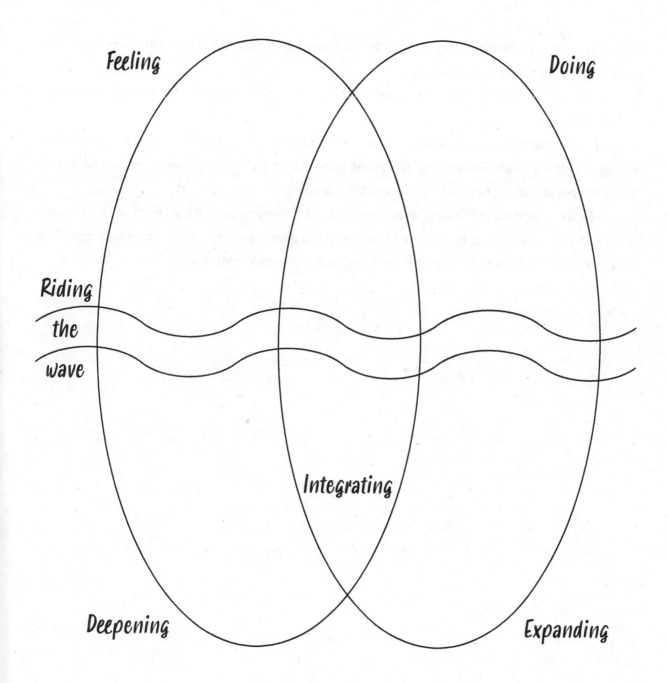

Feeling

Doing

Riding

the

wave

Integrating

Deepening

Expanding

PUT GRIEF DOWN—FOR A LITTLE WHILE

Sometimes it is necessary to put grief aside for a while. Grief is often all-consuming and exhausting, and takes a lot of energy.

It is okay to step away from the emotions, the ruminating and intrusive thoughts, in order to regroup.

Self-care is important when a person is overwhelmed by grief and the changes it has wrought in their lives. Separating different aspects of the grief experience can help the bereaved person identify what to put aside for a while.

Invite the client to reflect on their emotions and thoughts, writing them in the clouds. What can they do to keep busy for a while, perhaps getting some things done while setting their grief aside? What self-care and soothing activities can they do?

PUT GRIEF DOWN—FOR A LITTLE WHILE

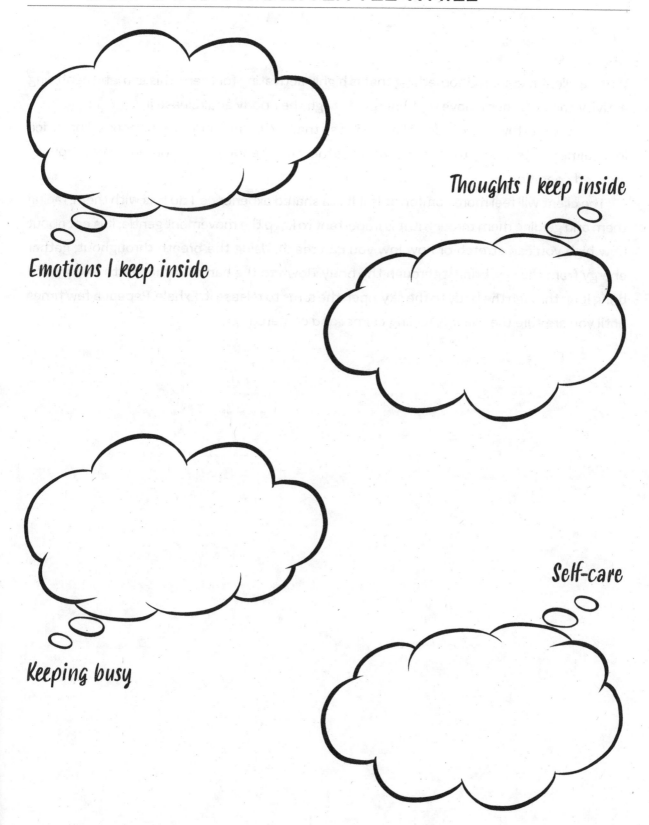

Emotions I keep inside

Thoughts I keep inside

Keeping busy

Self-care

CENTERING

When a client has shared something that is highly activating for them, this somatic centering activity can help them move that energy through their body and release it.

This is useful towards the end of a session so that the client can leave the counseling office in a calmer state, ready to face the world, rather than sending them out in an emotionally aroused condition.

The client will feel more comfortable if it is a shared experience. I do this with them, facing them and guiding them through it. It is important to keep the movement gentle; it is not about how high you can stretch or how low you can reach. Using the breath throughout, gather energy from the sky, bring it through the body, down to the earth. Gather earth energy and bring it up through the body to the sky, open the arms to release it. Exhale. Repeat a few times until you are sure the client is feeling calmer and centered.

CENTERING

Stand up. Take three deep breaths. Allow your breath to flow through your center. Feel yourself steady, grounded, arms relaxed. Breathe.

Slowly reach your arms up, stretching, looking up. Breathe in. On the exhale, open your arms and spread them wide.

Reach down towards the ground, touching it if possible. Do not stress your body, move gently within your own range of motion. Breathe.

Gather energy from the earth and bring it through your body, reaching up to the sky. Release at the top then gather again, down through your body. Breathe.

Repeat, reaching, gathering through your body, connecting you to sky and earth.
Keep breathing.

Stand quietly. Breathe.

TRACKING INTERNAL RESPONSES ▬▬▬▬▬▬

This activity tracks the polyvagal state and its fluctuations. The diagram can be used to focus on the internal nervous state the client is in at the moment. Invite the client to track their internal states and write them on the activity sheet.

This sheet can also be used to track the movement between dorsal, sympathetic, and ventral states through the course of a day by giving it to the client for homework. They might notice how their nervous system activates to keep them safe. They might notice what helps them move out of an uncomfortable feeling of fight, flight, or freeze.

Whether they are completing this activity in the counseling session or taking it home for deeper reflection, the client can also notice what "glimmers" help them move to a ventral, more connected, state. They can notice how they feel in the three polyvagal states, and see if they can apply thoughts, statements, or actions that help them recover and stay in a central state more often.

TRACKING INTERNAL RESPONSES

Notice the state of your nervous system. Are you in freeze, flight or fright? When do you feel calm and connected?

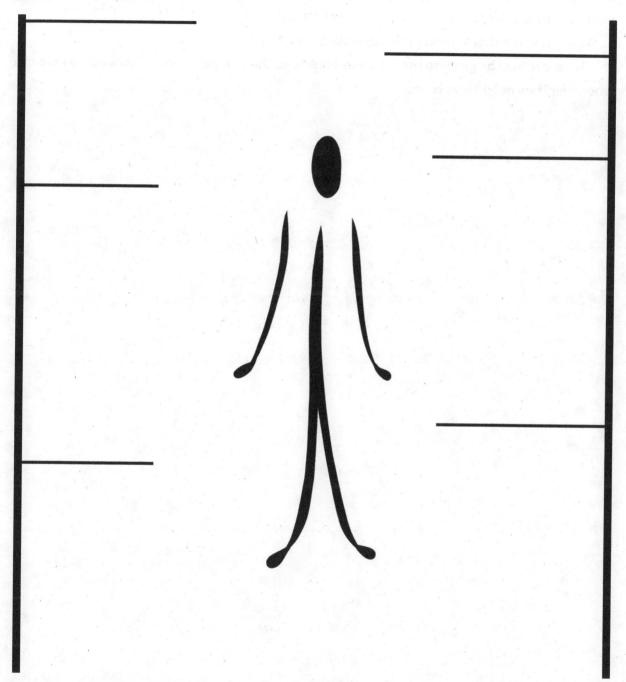

GROUNDING

This somatic activity can be used after a client has ventilated a lot of emotion. It can be used at the end of a session to help the client regulate any residual activation they may be feeling, so that they can leave your office in a calmer state.

You can guide them through this and do it with them.

The sheet may be given to them as a reference so that they can do this grounding exercise whenever they need to, at home.

GROUNDING

Sit in a comfortable chair with your feet flat on the ground. Sit relaxed but with your back straight. Place your hands on your knees or in your lap.

Inhale deeply, gently. Exhale slowly. Let your exhale be slightly longer than your inhale. Close your eyes if you wish.

Repeat, inhale, exhale. Feel your body, sitting on the chair, and your whole body breathing. In and out. In and out.

After a few cycles, place one hand on your belly and the other on your heart. Continue breathing. In and out. In and out.

Place your hands back on your knees.

Breathe. Feel your body, sitting in this chair, in this room.

Slowly open your eyes.

Turn up the corners of your mouth as you look around with a small smile.

✘

BANDS ▬▬▬▬▬▬▬▬▬▬▬▬▬▬▬▬▬▬▬▬▬▬▬▬

This acronym is a simple grounding technique to help calm and regulate emotions.

One of the problems in life is that we tend to project ourselves into the future and disengage from the present. In grief this is especially hard to cope with because often, a grieving person feels as if their future has evaporated.

By focusing on the present, applying *breath* and *attention*, the client can let go of those projections into the unknown. The acronym can be applied whenever they are feeling out of control or overly emotional in places where it is not safe to cry or express their grief. BANDS can become an activity they can do at their desk at work, on a train, or in any venue where they need a reminder to stay in the moment.

Engage the client with BANDS in your office and give them a reminder sheet for them to take home.

BANDS

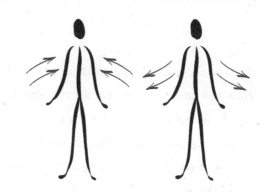

Breathe—Inhale slowly on a count of 4. Exhale on a count of 6. Repeat. Notice how your breath fills your body.

Attend to your needs—Listen. What do you need right now? Treat yourself gently.

Narrow your focus—Try not to think too far. Yesterday has passed, tomorrow is not here.

Draw on your inner resources—You have the ability to calm yourself. You have skills and resilient qualities that are unique to you. Remind yourself of your own resources.

Stay in the moment—There is only this moment. Stay in it, attending to your needs, attending to your breath.

SWING FROM THE SKY

This is an energizing somatic activity. It is useful for releasing pent-up energy and moving feelings and tension stuck in the body.

Be mindful of the client's capacity for movement. This activity can be done on a smaller or larger scale depending on what you are trying to help the client move. Keep it within their range of motion and be sure to move furniture away so that you both have space to swing from the sky.

If possible, go outside with your client to swing from the sky.

SWING FROM THE SKY

Stand straight and reach your arms up over your head. Inhale, bend your knees and exhale as you swing your arms down behind you. Let your head and back follow.

Straighten your knees and reach back. Inhale and swing back up, following your arms until you reach the top. Inhale and imagine that you are hanging from the sky.

Exhale as you swing back down. Inhale as you swing up and hang from the sky. Repeat.

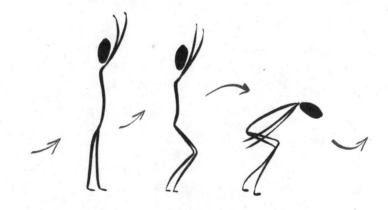

Continue to swing at your own pace, fast or slow, feeling the spring through your knees and back. Don't push, just breathe and swing from the sky.

STAR OF GRATITUDE

Focusing on gratitude is a good way to cope with the negative aspects of grief. It can be effective to list several things that you are grateful for at the end of the day. The gratitude statements can be small things, such as being grateful for the sun or the beauty observed in nature. You can be grateful for a phone call from a relative or a friend or for a nourishing meal or a lovely cup of tea.

Invite the client to use this starburst to write down what they are grateful for. They can use the circle to focus on connection with other people who are there for them and the outer bursts for things that bring gratitude to their lives.

They may also use the inner circle to express gratitude towards the person they are grieving. The outer bursts can be filled in with gratitude towards themselves, what they do well, how they are coping with their grief.

This star image is flexible, so present it as you wish. At first, the client may have difficulty finding things to be grateful for. Remind them to keep these small; little starbursts of gratitude can become glimmers of hope during their grief.

STAR OF GRATITUDE

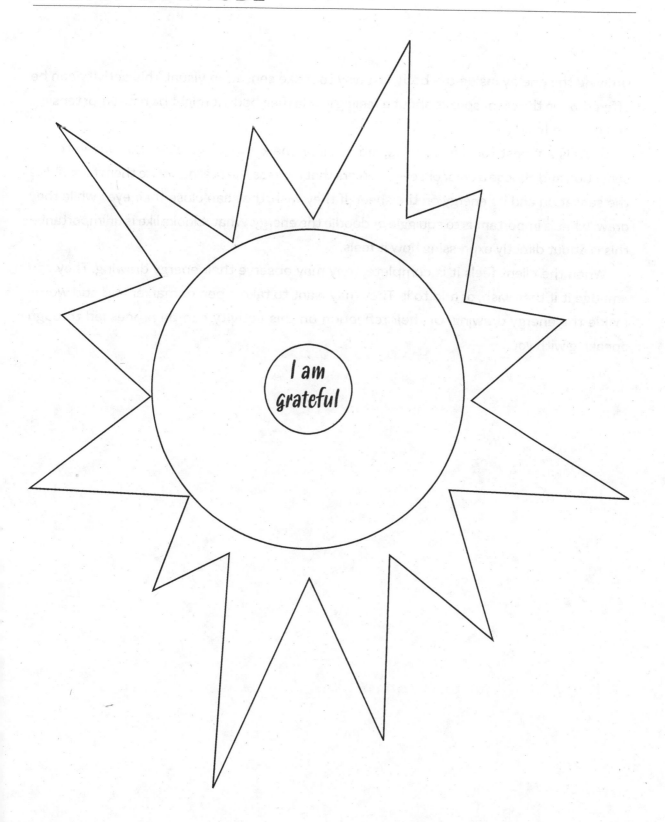

I am grateful

ENERGY DRAWING

Drawing the energy inside the body is a way to make sensation visual. This activity can be offered when the client speaks about a feeling inside their body. It might be nausea, or tension, or a buzzing feeling.

Pastels are best for this exercise, either oil or chalk. Invite the client to tune in to the sensation and choose a color or several colors that express the feeling. Invite them to scribble the sensation and its energy on the sheet. If they wish, they can close their eyes while they draw; what is important is to squiggle or doodle the energy. What it looks like is unimportant—this is about directly expressing how it feels.

When the client feels it is complete, they may observe their energy drawing. They can smudge it if they wish, or add to it. They may want to take a pen or marker and add words inside the energy drawing. Or their reflection on this activity can be processed through speaking with you.

ENERGY DRAWING

FEAR AND ACTION

Fear is a big part of grief. When the world appears shattered, everything can feel scary.

This diagram allows the client to explore what they fear. By writing it down and identifying it, fear doesn't have as much power.

After the client has identified their fears, they can focus on what they wish for. This section may not be realistic, but that is okay. Ask the client to write down what they wish and how they wish things could be.

Next, the client moves on to explore what they can do. This might be what they could do to alleviate their fear or what part of their wishing could perhaps be manifested.

After the diagram is complete, you can process it with the client. There is also an area at the bottom for reflection.

FEAR AND ACTION

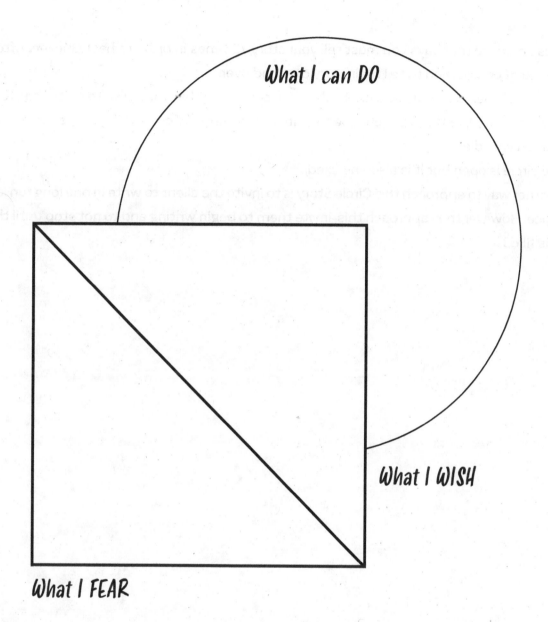

What I can DO

What I WISH

What I FEAR

Reflect on this process when you are finished with this activity:

_____

_____

_____

_____

CIRCLE STORY

There is an adage that says you must tell your story 72 times in order to heal. Grievers often feel a kind of compulsion to tell their story over and over.

By writing their story within a circle, they can contain it. They may wish to write the story of what happened, or they may choose to write a short story of something they shared with the person who died.

The circle is open but it is also enclosed.

Another way to approach this Circle Story is to invite the client to write in one long run-on sentence. However they approach this, invite them to begin writing and to not stop until the circle is filled.

CIRCLE STORY

✘

SPIRAL OF LOVE ▪▪▪▪▪▪▪▪▪▪▪▪▪

We grieve because we have loved. The purpose of this activity is to highlight love in the various ways that it shows up in our lives.

Invite the client to reflect on love. How are they lovable? How do they offer love and to whom? How do they receive love?

Ask the client to write their reflections within the spiral.

SPIRAL OF LOVE

SHIELD OF PROTECTION

The grieving person may have expectations about who will be there for them. It is often surprising that some of the people they believe should be there are unable to do so.

When a close relative or friend is not available to provide support or when they actively judge the griever or give unhelpful messages or bromides, it can be very disappointing.

There are relationships that ought to be close but that are not. These might feel toxic to the griever and it is hard for them to let go of what they wish to receive from these people.

What will protect the griever from toxic messages?

This activity can be done with drawing or with collage. The invitation is to draw or collage images and words that are protective and empowering for the client.

If you decide to use collage, you will need magazine images and colored paper. Glue sticks are the easiest to use for this. Stickers, feathers, or other materials can also be used. The client can bring in photographs or other images they wish to use.

Magazines and newspapers will yield words that the client can use or you can offer them pens or markers so that they can write their own words on their shield.

SHIELD OF PROTECTION

SELF-CARE PYRAMID

Taking care of yourself is hard for a grieving person to do. Whether they feel numb or extremely sad, anxious, or fearful, so much energy is expended. Grief creates worry, lack of sleep, and forgetfulness.

Noticing healthy and helpful ways to take care of oneself is useful. This pyramid is divided into sections to facilitate different ways to practice self-care:

- Sleep: How is the client sleeping? What self-care techniques can be applied to help them sleep better?

- Body: How are they taking care of their body? This could include nourishment, identifying teas or other beverages that they like. It may also include what to wear. Some bereaved people find their skin is sensitive—especially widowed people. They may find that wearing soft, loose clothing makes them feel a bit better.

- Soothing: What gentle things can they use to soothe themselves? This might include essential oils, bubble baths, listening to music, walking in nature, sitting outside. Or it might include journaling or drawing out how they feel.

- Connections: In terms of self-care, can the client identify who would be the most helpful, the easiest person to be with when they feel lonely or isolated? It may not be an obvious choice.

Invite the client to reflect on the various ways they can take care of their grieving self and write them in the parts of the pyramid. They can use the outside of the triangle to add other ways to self-care.

SELF-CARE PYRAMID

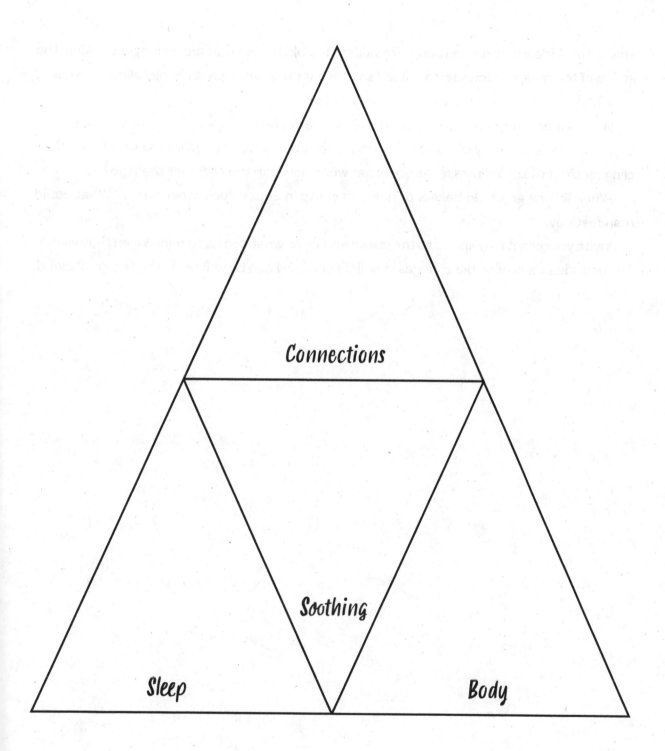

Connections

Soothing

Sleep

Body

CHALLENGING BELIEFS

This activity identifies rumination, core values, and old beliefs that are no longer working. The image of the face, sectioned into "what I say," "what I see," and "what I think," allows the client to reflect on how they share what they are ruminating on.

What aspects of their value system have been affected by death? How honest are they in their speech, or are they diplomatic in what they choose to say? What old beliefs are they clinging to? If these old messages no longer work, how can the client let them go?

When letting go of old beliefs or noticing shifts in core values, what arises? What could manifest now?

Invite your client to respond to the image and write what comes to mind when they view it. Any new ideas, any possible changes in beliefs or values can be written in the "I dream" cloud.

CHALLENGING BELIEFS

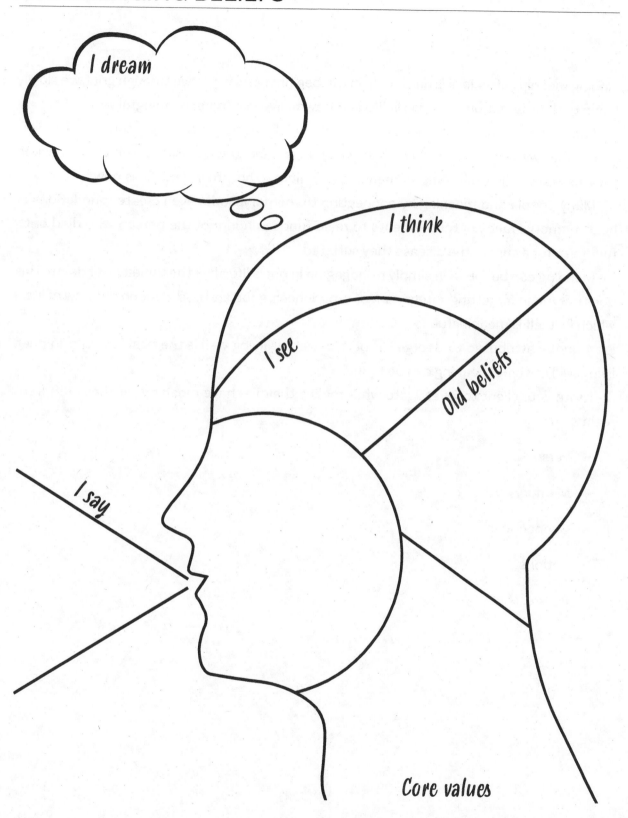

MEANING AND PURPOSE

Finding meaning after loss is hard to do in the beginning. As we move through grief, we slowly begin to think about our purpose in life and how to live in a more meaningful way.

Sometimes, meaning can be found by exploring the gifts received from the person who is gone. What we learned from them, how we changed and grew in relationship to them when they were alive can offer levels of meaning and hints to how to live our lives now.

Many people find meaning by connecting to memory. Some even create foundations or host memorial races or tournaments to raise funds in honor of the person who died or to fundraise for a cure of the disease they suffered.

Meaning can be found in simply re-engaging in one's life after the upheaval of death. This does not mean forgetting; integration of experiences, good and bad, deepen our view of life—which in itself is meaningful.

A quote, attributed to George Herbert, says that living well is the best revenge. In grief, living well is where meaning can be found.

Invite your client to investigate what makes their life have meaning for these different realms:

- Personal

- Memory

- Connections

- Actions

- Future.

MEANING AND PURPOSE

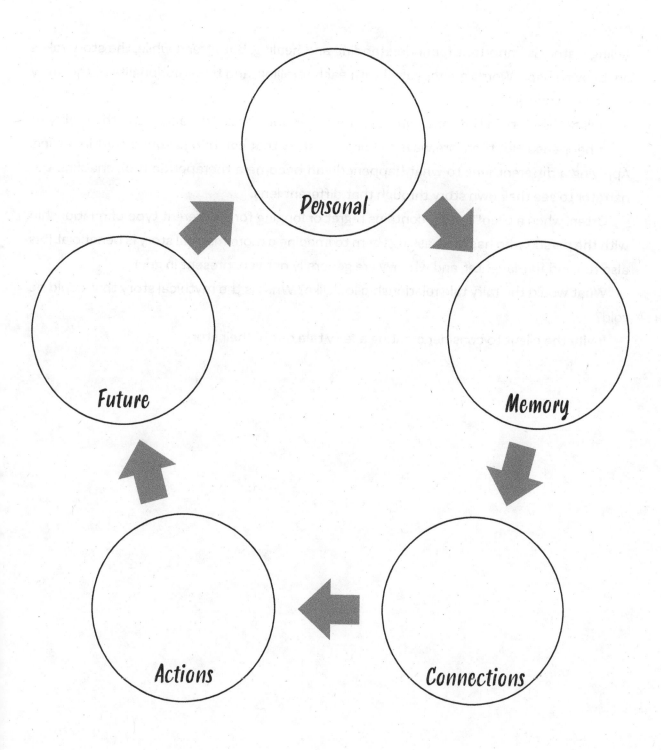

FAIRY TALE

Telling a story is important for understanding and healing, but after a while, the story takes on its own shape. Words are repeated with each retelling, and the emotionality of the story can lose its power.

Telling the story in the same way over and over does help with accepting the reality of what happened. But there are ways to tell one's story that can bring about a shift in feeling. Applying a different lens to what happened can become a therapeutic tool, enabling the narrator to see their own story through that different lens.

Often, when a client's story contains regret or longing for a different type of relationship with the person who has died, asking them to imagine a more magical story is beneficial. It is also fun and fun, laughter, and whimsy are generally not very present in grief.

What would the fairy tale relationship look like? What is the mythical story that could be told?

Invite the client to consider creating a fairy tale out of their story.

FAIRY TALE

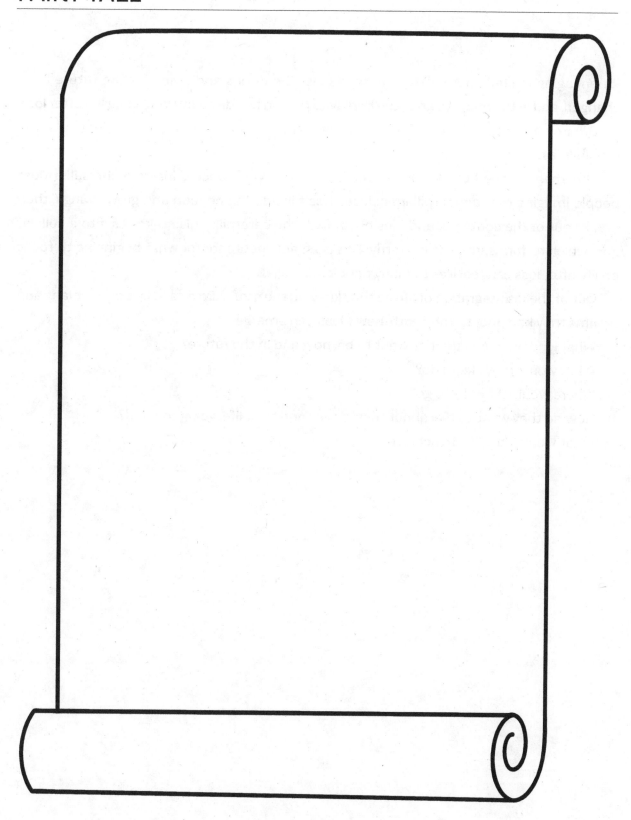

DREAMING THE FUTURE

Re-engaging in life is hard after someone dies. The hopes and plans for the future have changed, and in the midst of grief, the bereaved person has difficulty imagining life after loss.

Dreaming up ideas by considering specific areas of life may open the client to some possibilities.

The image of the butterfly is offered because of what occurs inside a chrysalis. Most people imagine that a caterpillar encloses itself inside the cocoon and grows wings, then breaks out of the container and flies off. In fact, the caterpillar disintegrates into a cellular goo, which re-forms into the butterfly. This is an apt metaphor for what beginning to focus on life after loss can feel like, to many people.

Out of the disintegration of life as they knew it, the structure exists. Out of the plans and dreams they had prior to the death, new ideas can emerge.

What kind of person do they want to be, now and in the future?

What would they like to do?

Where would they like to go?

How do they want to feel about themselves and their life, going forward?

What would they like to achieve?

DREAMING THE FUTURE

SHELL OF MEMORY ▮▮▮▮▮▮▮▮▮▮▮▮▮▮

In his book, *The Prophet* (2005), Kahlil Gibran says that pain is the shell that encloses understanding. People grieve and feel sorrow and pain after loss because they were connected to the person who died.

Love and pain are intrinsically joined. If we did not love, we would not grieve. Even in cases of difficult relationships, where the emotional reaction to the loss is complicated, perhaps by abuse, neglect, or basic incompatibility, the grieving person feels pain because of being connected.

Remembering can lead to understanding—who the person was, what they did in their life. Remembering aspects of the relationship can help the griever understand who they were relative to the person who died. Remembering fondly enhances the good in what was shared.

Invite the client to remember. Ask them to place word cues for several important memories. Discuss them, highlighting what was good, attempting to understand what may be uncomfortable.

SHELL OF MEMORY

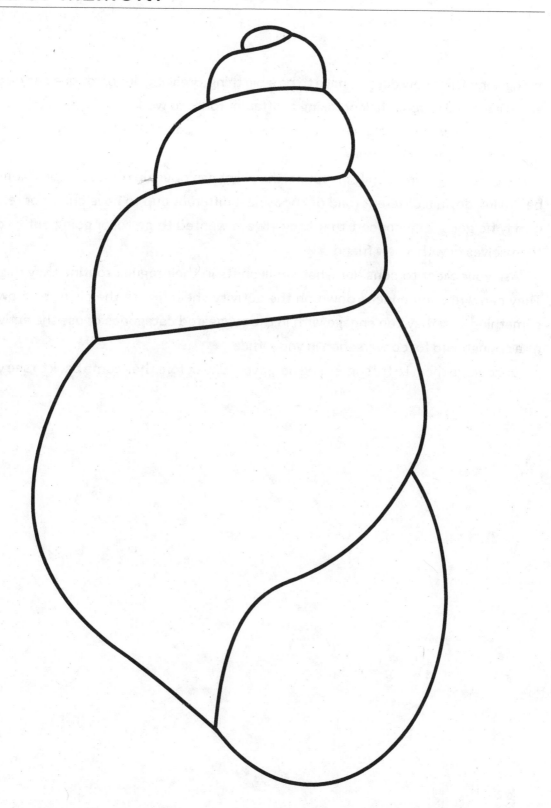

✗

TRY SOMETHING NEW ▐███████████████

Trying something new doesn't have to be a big thing. Breaking out of routine can be as simple as sitting in a different chair or taking a different route to work.

Trying a new routine can encourage the bereaved person to accept that change doesn't have to be a scary or bad thing.

By practicing a small shift in routine, the client can open up to possibilities. At first it may be driving down a different road or choosing a different cup to have coffee or tea in. Later, it may be going to a concert that they always wanted to go to, or going out to dinner by themselves or with a new friend.

Ask your client to consider what small shifts in their regular routine they might make. They can write some ideas down on the activity sheet. Invite the client to draw or write something new they can engage with in the suggested categories or use the activity sheet as a springboard for conversation in your office.

Encourage them to try something new every day before they come back to see you again.

New morning routine

Changing one small thing

Learning something new

Enjoying something different

Connecting with friends

✗

LOVE ▐▔▔▔▔▔▔▔▔▔▔▔▔▔▔▔▔▔▔▔▔▔▔▔▔▔▔

We grieve because we have loved, and often, in the midst of sorrow, a person forgets this. Guilt and regret can make them question whether they are lovable, and as they struggle to regain a sense of balance in their lives, they might wonder about their capacity for love.

This activity asks the bereaved client to focus on love. How do they offer love to another person? How did they show the deceased that they were loved?

How do they receive love? Did they receive love from the deceased, and how has this affected their sense of self?

What did they love about the person who is gone? What do they love about themselves?

Invite the client to focus on love and to feel it within their body, as if it is being generated from their heart and radiating through their center, out to their fingertips and toes. They might place their hands on their heart while they imagine themselves filling up with love.

Then, ask them to write down some words that express how they love, how they are loved, and why they are lovable.

LOVE

The love I give:

The love I receive:

I am lovable:

Resources

The following list contains links to websites of therapists, counselors, grief experts, and organizations that present information on end-of-life issues, death, and bereavement. I have also included several links where you can learn more about creative and expressive therapeutic techniques and interventions.

Please also refer to the References section that follows for specific titles cited in this book.

Association for Death Education and Counseling® (ADEC) provides education on thanatology, the study of death, dying, and bereavement. The Annual Conference presents current research along with experiential workshops demonstrating techniques and strategies currently in use. ADEC is a membership organization, and members have access to monthly webinars on various topics. ADEC is a credentialing organization and after meeting the study requirements, members may sit for an exam to be certified in thanatology. After six years of certification and a demonstration of continuing education and work in the field, there is an opportunity to become a Fellow in Thanatology:

www.adec.org/default.aspx

Hospice Foundation of America (HFA) seeks to "improve access, care and knowledge about hospice, loss and grief." It lobbies for better laws and regulations, and provides information on hospice care in the US, continuing education, and caregiver and grief support. HFA promotes conversation about end-of-life issues and palliative care, demystifying all aspects of death and dying:

https://hospicefoundation.org

Alexandra Kennedy, MA, MFT, is a transpersonal grief therapist who has many helpful books and also offers workshops and lectures. For more information, see:

www.alexandrakennedy.com

Dr Alan Wolfelt (Center for Loss & Life Transition®) is a grief therapist and author with an extensive list of grief books for all different types of loss. His *Healing Your Grieving Heart* books offer sensitive and practical ways to approach grief and include books for spousal loss, parental loss, sibling loss, and even grief reactions caused by divorce. Dr Wolfelt also has a guide for support groups and an accompanying journal. In addition to his books, Dr Wolfelt offers training and workshops, and his website also contains articles:

www.centerforloss.com/about-the-center-for-loss/about-dr-alan-wolfelt

David Kessler is a grief expert who worked closely with Elisabeth Kübler-Ross towards the end of her life and co-authored the book, *On Grief and Grieving*. His work on grief healing, his books, and his lectures and workshops have continued her work and expanded it:

https://davidkessler.org

Information on **Elisabeth Kübler-Ross** can be found on her Foundation page:

www.ekrfoundation.org

For information on Elisabeth Kübler-Ross's "five stages of grief," see:

https://grief.com/the-five-stages-of-grief

Dr Robert A. Neimeyer has been a driving force in thanatology research at the University of Memphis where he is a psychology professor. He lectures around the world and has authored books and worked on collections of essays with other therapists and counselors, focusing on effective and creative ways to help clients through grief. He maintains a section on his website where he answers questions from bereaved people. Dr Neimeyer is the director of the Portland Institute for Loss and Transition, and is concerned with how grieving people engage in meaning making after loss. For information about his work, his publications, and opportunities to hear him speak, visit:

www.robertneimeyerphd.com

Refuge in Grief is the website of therapist, widow, and author, Megan Devine. It contains a blog and resources for support, and also offers a 30-day writing program for grieving people. Refuge in Grief also presents podcasts:

www.refugeingrief.com

Heather Stang, MA, is a yoga therapist and meditation teacher as well as a thanatologist. On her Mindfulness & Grief podcast she interviews experts on the various ways they work with grieving people:

https://mindfulnessandgrief.com/category/podcast

CREATIVE RESOURCES

Deborah Koff-Chapin is an artist who created Touch Drawing, a simple but powerful monoprint technique. This process helps people explore their inner landscape, awakens creativity and has been used in many settings. Touch Drawing has been used in hospitals, mental health institutions, support groups, and individual counseling sessions. Deborah teaches all over the world and holds a week-long Gathering every July on Whidbey Island, Washington. Her drawings have been published in coloring books and in beautiful decks of Touch Drawing cards, called *Soul Cards*. These evocative images are useful in counseling. I invite clients to pick several cards, lay them out to view them, and then create a story relating to what they are coping with at the moment. Information about Touch Drawing, including demonstration videos, as well as information about workshops to attend, can be found at:

> https://touchdrawing.com

IEATA, the International Expressive Arts Therapy Association®, has many resources for training and workshops as well as certifications on its website. It promotes the use of expressive modalities in all aspects of life, for personal and professional use:

> www.ieata.org

OTHER HELPFUL ORGANIZATIONS AND FOUNDATIONS
In the US

Open to Hope:

> www.opentohope.com

The Compassionate Friends:

> www.compassionatefriends.org

The Dougy Center:

> www.dougy.org

The National Alliance for Grieving Children

> https://childrengrieve.org

In the UK

Child Bereavement UK:

> www.childbereavementuk.org

Cruse Bereavement Care:

www.cruse.org.uk

In Canada

Bereavement Ontario Network:

https://bereavementontarionetwork.ca

Hospice of the Northwest:

www.hospicenw.org

In Singapore

Academy of Human Development:

www.ahd.com.sg/index.php

References

Attig, T. (2011) *How We Grieve: Relearning the World*. New York: Oxford University Press.

Bowlby, J. (1977) 'The making and breaking of affectional bonds.' *The British Journal of Psychiatry 130*, 421–431.

Bowlby, J. and Parkes, C.M. (1970) 'Separation and Loss.' In E. Anthony and C. Kopernick (Eds) *The Child in His Family, Vol. 1, The International Yearbook of Child Psychiatry*. New York: Wiley.

Bulfinch, T. (1963) *Bulfinch's Mythology*. London: Spring Books.

Dana, D. (2018) *Polyvagal Theory in Therapy*. New York: W.W. Norton & Company.

Dass, R. (1971) *Be Here Now*. Cristobal, CO: Lama Foundation.

Devine, M. (2017) *It's OK that You're NOT OK*. Boulder, CO: Sounds True.

Doka, K.A. (2016) *Grief Is a Journey*. New York: Atria.

Frankl, V.E. (2006) *Man's Search for Meaning*. Boston, MA: Beacon Press.

Freud, S. (1953) 'Mourning and Melancholia.' In J. Strachey (ed.) *The Standard Edition of the Complete Psychological Works of Sigmund Freud*, Vol. XIV (pp.237–258). London: Hogarth Press.

Gibran, K. (2005) *The Prophet*. New York: Alfred A. Knopf.

Kübler-Ross, E. (1969) *On Death and Dying: What the Dying Have to Teach Doctors, Nurses, Clergy and Their Own Families*. London: Tavistock.

Kübler-Ross, E. and Kessler, D. (2005) *On Grief and Grieving: Finding the Meaning of Grief through the Five Stages of Loss*. London: Simon & Schuster.

Kumar, S. (2005) *Grieving Mindfully: A Compassionate and Spiritual Guide to Coping with Loss*. Oakland, CA: New Harbinger Publications.

Lichtenthal, W.G. and Neimeyer, R.A. (2012) 'Directed Journaling to Facilitate Meaning Making.' In R.A. Neimeyer (ed.) *Techniques of Grief Therapy: Creative Practices for Counseling the Bereaved* (pp.165–168). New York: Routledge.

Lindemann, E. (1944) 'Symptomology and management of acute grief.' *American Journal of Psychiatry 101*, 2, 141–148.

McNiff, S. (1998) *Trust the Process: An Artist's Guide to Letting Go*. Boston, MA: Shambhala.

Neimeyer, R.A. (2012) 'Presence, Process and Procedure: A Relational Frame for Technical Proficiency in Grief Therapy.' In R.A. Neimeyer (ed.) *Techniques of Grief Therapy: Creative Practices for Counseling the Bereaved* (pp.3–11). New York: Routledge.

Parkes, C.M. (1987) 'Models of bereavement care.' *Death Studies 11*, 4, 257–261.

Parkes, C.M. and Prigerson, H.G. (2010) *Bereavement: Studies of Grief in Adult Life*. London: Penguin.

Pennebaker, J.W. (1997) *Opening Up: The Healing Power of Expressing Emotions*. New York: The Guilford Press.

Pennebaker, J.W. and Evans, J.F. (2014) *Expressive Writing: Words that Heal*. Eumenclas, WA: Idyll Arbor, Inc.

Rosenfeld, E.K. (2018) 'The fire that changed the way we think about grief.' *The Harvard Crimson*, November 29. Accessed on 29/11/2019 at www.thecrimson.com/article/2018/11/29/erich-lindemann-cocoanut-grove-fire-grief

SARK (2010) *Glad No Matter What: Transforming Loss and Change into Gift and Opportunity*. Novato, CA: New World Library.

Stang, H. (2018) *Mindfulness and Grief*. London: CICO Books.

Stroebe, M. and Schut, H. (2013) 'The dual process model of coping and with bereavement: Rationale and description.' *Death Studies 23*, 3, 197–224.

Strouse, S. (2013) *Artful Grief.* Bloomington, IN: Balboa Press.

Tedeschi, R.G., Shakespeare-Finch, J., Taku, K. and Calhoun, L.G. (2018) *Posttraumatic Growth: Theory, Research and Application.* New York: Routledge.

Wolfelt, A.D. (2003) *Understanding Your Grief: Ten Essential Touchstones for Finding Hope and Healing Your Heart.* Fort Collins, CO: Companion Press.

Worden, J.W. (2009) *Grief Counseling and Grief Therapy: A Handbook for the Mental Health Practitioner*, Fourth edn. New York: Springer Publishing Company.

Worden, J.W. (2018) *Grief Counseling and Grief Therapy: A Handbook for the Mental Health Practitioner*, Fifth edn. New York: Springer Publishing Company.

Index